T0165447

BIOENERGETICS

A novel theory for ATP synthesis

Baltazar D. Reynafarje

The Johns Hopkins University School of Medicine
Department of Biological Chemistry
Baltimore, MD USA

Order this book online at www.trafford.com
or email orders@trafford.com

Most Trafford titles are also available at major online book retailers.

Printed in the United States of America.

ISBN: 978-1-4907-1380-9 (Softcover)
ISBN: 978-1-4907-1382-3 (Hardcover)
ISBN: 978-1-4907-5210-5 (Audio)
ISBN: 978-1-4907-1381-6 (e-Book)

Library of Congress Control Number: 2013916420

Trafford rev. 01/08/2015

www.trafford.com

North America & international
toll-free: 1 888 232 4444 (USA & Canada)
fax: 812 355 4082

This book is dedicated with much love to my youngest grandsons
Wesley Salomon and Alberto Lorenzo

PREFACE

This book is designed to provide new trends of thought concerning the transformations of energy occurring in the life of humans, which in accordance with the basic laws of thermodynamics inexorably lead to a state of equilibrium and minimal potential energy. Under physiological conditions, life proceeds *far from equilibrium* maintaining a highly organized, structured and constrained state that apparently violates the second law of thermodynamics, which states that the *entropy* of the universe is *constantly* increasing. Life, however, is an ephemeral phenomenon that only exists due to the free energy that is brought into being by increasing the entropy of the environment so that the *total energy of the universe remains constant*. Thus, the energy utilized in the synthesis of ATP, which is the universal currency of free energy in living cells, begins not with a sudden increment in the level of ADP but with the binding of O_2 to mitochondria already charged with both respiratory substrates and ADP. In fact, the provision of free energy that is involved in the traffic of ions and metabolites and the homeostasis of the cell is tightly regulated by the *in vivo* concentration of O_2. Consequently, the reduction of O_2 to water and the synthesis of ATP were described in this book by analyzing the kinetics and thermodynamics of O_2 uptake and ATP synthesis that takes place from the beginning to the end of the process of oxidative phosphorylation. Pertinent aspects of general and comparative physiology are described to shed light on the mechanism of energy generation occurring under normal and pathological conditions. We hope that this book will help researchers to find alterations in energy metabolism not only by determining the genetic code of the cell but also by simply determining the processes of O_2 consumption and ATP synthesis.

CONTENTS

SECTION I

ENERGY TRANSFORMATIONS IN LIVING ORGANISMS

I. 1. Introduction

The central theme of bioenergetics has to do with the principles that govern the transformations of energy in living organisms. Energy, i.e. the ability of matter to perform work as the results of motion or position, exists in various forms, including mechanical, thermal, chemical, electrical, radiant, and atomic. All forms of energy, except *entropy*, may be converted to other forms of energy. *Kinetic energy* (the energy related with motion) and *potential energy* (the energy related to position) may be lost or gained, but the total of the two remains constant.

The concept of equivalence between mass and energy refers to the physical principle establishing that a measured quantity of *energy* (*E*) is equivalent to a measured quantity of *mass* is expressed by the following Einstein's equation:

$$E = mc^2 = (ma).d \tag{1}$$

In this form of kinetic energy, m is the unified body of *mass* that occupies space, a is the acceleration applied to m, d is the distance

1

through which a acts, and c is the speed of light. This concept, however, only holds true for events involving velocities equal to the velocity of light. For velocities lower than the speed of light the value of E can be derived from the following equation:

$$E = \tfrac{1}{2}\, mv^2 \tag{2}$$

where v^2 is the speed multiplied by itself. At higher velocities close to that of light energy and matter are interconvertible.

Living organisms require a continual input and utilization of free energy for three main purposes: the performance of *dynamical energy* for cellular motion; the active transport of molecules and ions; and the synthesis of macromolecules from simple precursors. The free-energy that sustains life on both *phototropic and chemotropic organisms,* comes from solar energy. In plants and photosynthetic bacteria, the protein complexes in charge to make available the quanta of visible light are contained in *chloroplasts.* In aerobic organisms, the protein complexes in charge to make available the free energy of electron flow towards oxygen are contained in the mitochondria of eukaryotic organisms and the membranes of cyanobacteria and prokaryotic cells

Although the number of protein-assemblies that exists inside the cell is overwhelmingly large, the number of assemblies involved in the synthesis of ATP, which is the *universal form of free energy in living organisms,* is relatively small. The essential elements that, together with O_2, CO_2, ADP and P_i, are involved in the oxidative phosphorylation process of ATP synthesis are the electrons and protons contained in highly reduced respiratory substrates. The protein complexes in charge to catalyze the *downhill* or exergonic flow of electrons towards O_2 and the *uphill* or endergonic synthesis of ATP from ADP and P_i are localized in the inner mitochondrial membrane of eukaryotes.

I. 2. Basic laws of thermodynamics

All biological reactions that occur in nature are subject to the universal laws of thermodynamics. Although cells are open systems that are never at equilibrium, a description of the principles of equilibrium thermodynamics (as applied to ordinary chemical reactions) is necessary to understand that the work done by the cell always takes place under conditions that are far from equilibrium. Thermodynamics is the field of physics that deals with the relationship between heat and other forms of energy such as pressure, temperature and volume. Everything that happens in living organisms is subject to the laws of thermodynamics.

The first law of thermodynamics is the law of energy conservation. It states that energy can neither be created nor destroyed. In any given process, one form of energy may be converted into another but the total energy of the system (the cell) plus its environment remains constant. The total energy of the *universe is constant.* Whatever its nature (thermal, chemical, electrical, mechanical, kinetic, potential, or atomic), the energy is neither created nor destroyed; it is only transformed and distributed between the system and its universe. A system in a given state has a definite amount of *internal energy,* i.e. the total kinetic and potential energy associated with the motions and relative positions of *the molecules of an object, excluding the kinetic or potential energy of the object as a whole* (the system and its environment). A rise in temperature or change in phase of the system, results in a rise of *internal energy,* generally represented by U. The internal energy can be changed in only two ways: (1) heat energy can flow into or out of the system, and (2) the system can do work of some kind against external forces. Thus,

$$\Delta U = \Delta Q - \Delta W \qquad (3)$$

where ΔU is the *general representation of the change in internal energy of the system*, ΔQ is the heat that flow into or out of the system, and ΔW is the work (quantity equal to the force applied to an object time the motion of the object in direction of the applied force) done by the system. By convention, ΔW *appears with a negative sign because any work done by the system reduces its internal energy.* In reactions in which there is a change in the electrical or oxidation-reduction potential of the system *the change in internal energy* (ΔE) is mathematically expressed by the following equation:

$$\Delta E\ (E_B - E_A) = \Delta Q - \Delta W \qquad (4)$$

in which E_A is the energy of the system at the start of the process and E_B the energy of the system at the end of the process. The sign of ΔE depends on the extent of heat that flows into or out of the system. When the heat that flows into the system (ΔQ) increases the internal energy increases and the sign of ΔE in equation 4 is positive.

The first law of thermodynamics is simply a law of conservation of energy. Nothing is said about the relative usefulness, direction or spontaneity of the reaction. Some reactions do occur spontaneously even when ΔE is positive, i.e. when the free energy of the system increases. In such cases, the system absorbs heat from its surroundings and the *entropy (S)* or degree of randomness or disorder of the system decreases.

The second law of thermodynamics states that *all naturally occurring processes proceed toward equilibrium, i.e. in the direction of minimal potential energy.* These so-called *spontaneous reactions* release energy that can be harnessed, transformed and made to do work. A more complete statement of the second law of thermodynamics includes the concept of entropy (S), which in a closed thermodynamic system is a quantitative measure of the amount of thermal energy not available to do work. Thus, in accordance with the second law of thermodynamics a reaction can occur spontaneously only if the sum of the *entropies* of the system and its surrounding increase or is higher than zero:

$$(\Delta S_{\text{system}} + \Delta S_{\text{surroundings}}) > 0 \qquad\qquad (5)$$

The more random, disordered, disorganized, or chaotic the system, the higher is the entropy. Spontaneous processes only occur when the entropy of the system and its environment increases. For example, the hydrolysis of ATP to P_i and ADP is thermodynamically feasible because the entropy of the system, ATP, is smaller than the entropy of P_i, ADP, and the surroundings. The energy lost by the hydrolysis of ATP (-7.3 kcal/mol) is lower than the actual energy required for its synthesis (ΔG = -12 kcal/mol). While the total energy of a system and its surrounding remains constant, the energy is distributed in a quantitatively different way after a spontaneous reaction.

The second law of thermodynamics, however, says nothing about the extent and relative utility of the transformations of energy. If matter and energy can only go from a state of maximal organization to a state of *inert uniformity, maximal disorganization and chaos*, how then can we explain the very existence of life, the quality that distinguishes highly organized matter from inanimate and disorganized matter? Life, however, does not violate any law of thermodynamics. The natural tendency of matter and energy in a given organism to run downhill can be counteracted by putting energy or doing work on the organism. In any particular system the energy may increase, remain constant or decrease while the total energy of the system, i.e. the energy of the system receiving the energy plus that of the system providing the energy, remains constant. A more complete statement of the second law that takes into account the single-directionality of spontaneous processes and the decreased potential to do further work is this: *"the entropy of the universe is constantly increasing"*.

The third law of thermodynamics states that at a temperature of absolute zero ($0°K$), where all random motion ceases, the entropy of a perfect crystal is zero, that is, all the atoms are maximally organized. However, if in accordance with the laws of thermodynamics the randomness or disorder of the universe is constantly increasing, do we have to assume that the universe was at some time a perfect crystal? Consider the adequacy of the Big Bang theory.

I. 3. Endergonic, exergonic, and Gibbs free energy change in living organisms

Living cells are exceedingly complex and delicate structures that grow and multiply maintaining their integrity over long periods of time by utilizing the energy contained in "energy-rich compounds". Chemical reactions that yield free energy and are capable of doing work are called *"exergonic"*. Those that utilize energy and need work to be done in order to proceed are called *"endergonic"*. Seldom, however, the free energy released by an exergonic reaction is directly transferred to an endergonic reaction. In general, the free energy released during exergonic reactions is conserved through a series of coupled reactions until the final endergonic reaction takes place. For example, the free energy released during the exergonic oxidation of respiratory substrates, is first transformed into the free energy of electron flow which eventually is utilized in the endergonic process of ATP synthesis.

Even though the *entropy of the universe is constantly increasing*, exergonic and endergonic reactions in closed thermodynamic systems can apparently happen *"spontaneously"*. One difficulty in using entropy to define a *spontaneous reaction* is that the entropy is practically impossible to measure (see equation 4). This difficulty is obviated by using the concept of free energy change or *Gibbs free energy change (ΔG)*, as represented by the following equation:

$$\Delta G = \Delta H - T\Delta S \tag{6}$$

In this equation, ΔG is the change in free energy of a system undergoing transformation at constant pressure (P) and temperature (T), ΔH is the *change in enthalpy or heat content of the system*, and ΔS is the change in entropy,

$$\Delta H = \Delta E + P\Delta V \qquad (7)$$

Because the volume-change (ΔV) in almost every biochemical reaction is very small and ΔH *is nearly equal to* ΔE, the change in free energy of the system (ΔG) can be approximately represented by the following equation:

$$\Delta G = \Delta E - T\Delta S \qquad (8)$$

A reaction can occur spontaneously only when the change in entropy or disorder in the system ($T\Delta S$,) increases above the energy content of the system (ΔE) and the ΔG is negative. If the ΔG is positive the reaction will not occur spontaneously unless an input of free energy from a coupled reaction drives the system towards equilibrium. When a physical system *moves* from one state of equilibrium to another, a thermodynamic process is said to take place. This phenomenon is divided into the part being studied, the *system*, and the region around the system, the *surroundings*. Whenever work is done on an object, there is a transfer of energy to the object, and so work is considered to be *energy in transit*. If a constantly acting force does not produce motion there is no work performed. For example, steadily holding an object above the floor does not involve any work, but the energy used to lift the object from the floor is retained in the object. This energy is released only when the object falls to the floor. The energy *released or utilized* in a chemical reaction at constant temperature and pressure is called *free energy difference*, ΔG, or Gibbs free energy change. The ΔG of a chemical reaction represents the difference between the ratio of products and substrates *at the beginning of the reaction* and the ratio of products and substrates *at equilibrium*.

$$\Delta G = \text{[actual product/substrate ratios]} -$$
$$\text{[product/substrate ratios at equilibrium]} \qquad (9)$$

More specifically, in the reaction from A and B (substrates) to C and D (products)

$$\Delta G = actual\ RT\ ln\ [C]^c\ [D]^d\ /\ [A]^a\ [B]^b\ -$$
$$RT\ ln\ [C]^c\ [D]^d\ /\ [A]^a\ [B]^b\ at\ K'_{eq} \qquad (10)$$

Where R is the gas constant = 1.987 cal mole^{-1} $^{\circ}$K^{-1},
    T is the absolute temperature, $^{\circ}$K at 25°C = 298°K,
    and a, b, c, d = coefficients of A, B, C and D, respectively.

In accordance with equations 8 and 9 figure I-1 illustrates how the value of ΔG controls the direction of a reaction. Thus, when [S] >> [P] and ΔG is negative, i.e., when the *actual RT ln [P] / [S]* is lower than the *RT ln [P] / [S]* at equilibrium, the reaction can take place spontaneously.

$- \Delta G$ $\qquad\qquad$ $\Delta G = 0$ $\qquad\qquad$ $+ \Delta G$

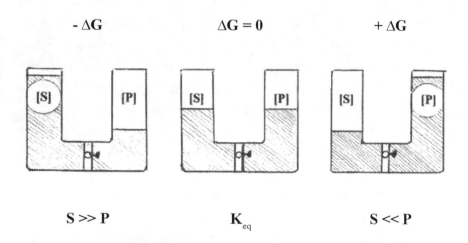

$S >> P$ $\qquad\qquad$ K_{eq} $\qquad\qquad$ $S << P$

Figure I-1. The sign of ΔG controls the direction in the flow of substrates and products [After I.H. Segel. *Biochemical calculations*, 2nd edition (1974): 151]

The reaction will proceed "spontaneously" only when the concentration of the substrate is higher than the concentrations of product and ΔG is negative. When the *actual concentration* of product is higher than the *actual concentration* of substrate and the ΔG is positive, the reaction will never occur spontaneously. Whatever the membrane potential (ΔE_m) or the redox potential (ΔE_h), the free energy change (ΔG) of a reaction and its sign is a valuable criterion to know the *direction in which the energy metabolism of the cell proceeds.*

The value of ΔG tells how far the reaction is from equilibrium but says *absolutely nothing about the rate at which the reaction approaches equilibrium.* Many reactions with very large negative ΔG values do not proceed at detectable rates in the absence of appropriate conditions. The ΔG can predict three important aspects of a reaction. (1) A reaction takes place spontaneously only if ΔG is negative. (2) The value of ΔG in a reaction at equilibrium is zero and no net change in energy occurs in any direction. (3) A reaction cannot take place spontaneously if ΔG is positive. Reactions with a positive ΔG require an input of free energy to be driven. Thus, under *absolute resting conditions*, when the ΔE_h and the concentrations of O_2, ADP and P_i are very high, the rates of O_2 uptake and ATP synthesis will not occur at fast rates if the mitochondria and cytochrome aa_3 are for the most part oxidized. Remember that ΔG only indicates the *difference* between the free energy contents of the products and the original substrates and that the magnitude of ΔG is independent of the path and the number of steps involved in the generation of the final product.

A fundamental statement in bioenergetics is that the *changes in free energy of coupled reactions are additive* and that a reaction with a negative ΔG can drive a non-spontaneous reaction with a positive $\Delta G^{o'}$. Data in Figure I-2 demonstrate that in coupled reactions the over all values of ΔG and K_{eq} are the same regardless of the number of steps involved in the transformations of S to P, i.e.

$$\Delta G_5 = \Delta G_1 + \Delta G_3 = \Delta G_2 + \Delta G_4$$

and
$$K_{eq5} = K_{eq1} \times K_{eq3} = K_{eq2} \times K_{eq4}$$

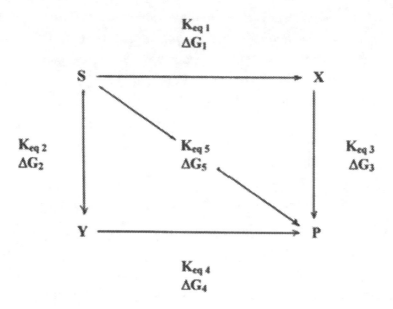

$$K_{eq\,1}$$
$$\Delta G_1$$

Figure I-2. The overall value of ΔG and K_{eq} in coupled reactions is the same [After I.H. Segel, in *Biochemical calculations*, 2nd edition (1974): 153]

I. 4. Relationship between free-energy change and equilibrium constant

To catalog and compare ΔG values for various reactions, chemists have agreed to consider a hypothetical *standard state* where all reactants and products are considered to be maintained at a steady state concentration of 1 M. When H^+ is a reactant, the standard state is defined as having a pH of 7.0 and its activity is given a value of 1.0. The standard-state for gases is considered to be 1 atmosphere partial pressure. Under these conditions the log [P]/[S] in the first term of equation 10 is zero, regardless of exponents.

$$RT \ln [C]^c [D]^d / [A]^a [B]^b = 0$$

and the symbol ΔG is represented by the symbol $\Delta G^{o'}$:

$$\Delta G^{o'} = 0 - RT \ln [C]^c [D]^d / [A]^a [B]^b \text{ at equilibrium} \tag{11}$$

Thus, at equilibrium (K'_{eq}) and 25°C or 298 °K, the standard free energy change of a reaction is related to its equilibrium constant, K'_{eq}, by the following expression.

$$\Delta G^{o'} = -1.363 \text{ Kcal/mole} \times K'_{eq} \tag{12}$$

For every order of magnitude in K'_{eq} the *value* of $\Delta G^{o'}$ changes by a factor of 1.363 Kcal/mole. In other words, the ability of a reaction to do work is directly related to the [product]/[substrate] ratio at equilibrium and to the sign of $\Delta G^{o'}$ (see Table I -1).

In fact, the values of ΔG^{o} and K'_{eq} impart the same information, i.e. the direction and how far a reaction will proceed when all substrates and products are 1M. The actual ΔG under any particular set of concentration can be calculated from:

$$\Delta G = 1364 \log [products] / [substrates] - 1364 \log K'_{eq} \tag{13}$$

Under standard conditions (when the pH is 7.0 and actual concentrations of reactants and products are equal to 1 M) the reaction will not occur spontaneously if the value of ΔG is positive (see Table I-1).

Remember that the value of ΔG is equal to the difference between the product to substrate ratio at any time and the product to substrate ratio at equilibrium (see equations 10 and 13). Although the standard fee-energy change $\Delta G^{o'}$ of a reaction maintains a definite correlation with its equilibrium constant, K_{eq}, *it is only when ΔG is negative that the reaction can take place spontaneously*. In other words, the criterion of spontaneity is given by ΔG not by $\Delta G^{o'}$.

Table I-1 Correlation between $\Delta G^{o'}$ and K'_{eq}

K'_{eq}	$\log K'_{eq}$	$\Delta G^{o'}$	
[P] / [S]		kcal/mol	kJ/mole
0.00001	-5	6.82	28.53
0.0001	-4	5.46	22.84
0.001	-3	4.09	17.11
0.01	-2	2.73	11.42
0.1	-1	1.36	5.69
1	0	0	0
10	1	-1.36	-5.59
100	2	-2.73	-11.42
1000	3	-4.09	-17.11
10000	4	-5.46	-22.84
100000	5	-6.82	-28.53

Consider, for example, the isomerization of dihydroxyacetone phosphate to glyceraldehyde 3-phosphate, which under standard conditions of 1 M, 25°C, and pH 7, has a K'_{eq} of 0.0475.

$$\Delta G^{o'} = -1.364 \text{ Kcal/mole} \times \log 0.0475$$
$$\Delta G^{o'} = -1.364 \times \text{Kcal/mole} \times -1.323 = +1.8 \text{ kcal/mol}$$

The value of ΔG can be calculated knowing the actual concentrations of the product (glyceraldehyde 3-phosphate) and substrate (dihydroxyacetone). Assuming, for example, that the product is equal to 1×10^{-6} M and the substrate is equal to 4×10^{-4} M, the value of ΔG would be:

$$\Delta G = \Delta G^{o'} - RT \log K'_{eq}$$
$$\Delta G = +1.84 \text{ kcal/mol} - 1.364 \log 1 \times 10^{-6} \text{ M} / 4 \times 10^{-4}$$
$$\Delta G = +1.84 \text{ kcal/mole} - 2.6 \text{ kcal/mol} = -0.76 \text{ kcal/mol}$$

Since under these particular conditions the ΔG of the isomerization of dihydroxyacetone phosphate to glyceraldehyde 3-phosphate is negative (-0.76 kcal/mol), the reaction can occur spontaneously even though the $\Delta G^{o'}$ is positive (+1.8 kcal/mole). We must repeat that the *extent and rates* of a reaction depend on the concentrations of the reactants and that the criterion of spontaneity is based on ΔG not $\Delta G^{o'}$

I. 5. Enthalpy and Entropy

The first and second laws of thermodynamics relate the ΔG of a reaction to the heat evolved in the following way:

$$\Delta G = \Delta H - T \Delta S$$

ΔH is called *enthalpy change*, and represents the quantity of heat releases (or absorbed) at constant temperature, pressure and volume. ΔS is the *entropy change* and is a measure of the change in the randomness of the system. Thus, the sum of the internal energy of the system plus the product of its volume multiplied by the pressure exerted on it by the surroundings is called *enthalpy*, i.e. $\Delta H = \Delta G + T \Delta S$

THERMODYNAMICALLY FAVORABLE AND UNFAVORABLE REACTIONS

II. 1. Introduction

The exceedingly complex structure of the cell is maintained *far from equilibrium* by using the free energy of solar energy in *phototropic organisms* and foodstuffs in *chemotropic organisms*. Cells do not only maintain their integrity over long periods of time but also grow and multiply *utilizing* the energy released from exergonic reactions with a highly negative $\Delta G^{o'}$. In fact, living organisms require a continual input of free energy to sustain three main functions: the synthesis of macromolecules from simple precursors, the dynamical process of cellular motion, and the active transport of molecules and ions across membranes. However, due to the fact that biological membranes are essentially impermeable to ions and metabolites, the transport of these molecules against concentration gradients is gated by a membrane potential or a covalent modification of the transport systems by *allosteric proteins*.

II. 2. The active transport of ions and metabolites requires the input of free energy

Living cells have the ability to transport and accumulate certain compounds against large concentration gradients in spite of the fact that these compounds have *per se* a positive $\Delta G^{o'}$. Seldom, however, the transformations of energy involve the simultaneous catalysis of two reactions. Because the transfer of *free energy in coupled reactions is additive* the energy released from an exergonic reaction is first trapped in energy reach compounds which then are used to support the performance of an endergonic reaction with a positive $\Delta G^{o'}$. Consider the three thermodynamically related reactions:

a) A to B $\qquad\qquad\qquad\qquad$ $\Delta G = + 4.0$ kcal/mol $\qquad$ (1)
b) $ATP = ADP + P_i$ $\qquad\qquad$ $\Delta G = - 7.3$ kcal/mol $\qquad$ (2)
c) $A + ATP = B + ADP + P_i$ $\qquad$ $\Delta G = - 3.3$ kcal/mol $\qquad$ (3)

The thermodynamically unfavorable reaction (1) with a $\Delta G^{o'}$ of + 4.0 cannot take place spontaneously unless it is coupled to an exergonic reaction (2) with a large negative ΔG such as the hydrolysis of ATP. The coupled transformation of A to B can now proceed because the overall ΔG is negative (3).

Under standard conditions the relationship between K_{eq} and ΔG, for reactions a, b and c is, respectively:

(a) $\Delta G = + 4.0$ kcal/mol $+ 1364 \ln K'_{eq}$
(b) $\Delta G = - 7.3$ kcal/mol $+ 1364 \ln K'_{eq}$
(c) $\Delta G = - 3.3$ kcal/mol $+ 1364 \ln K'_{eq}$

Also:

(a) K_{eq} for $([B] / [A]) = 10^{-4/1.364} = 1.17 \times 10^{-3}$
(b) K_{eq} for $([ADP] [P_i]/ [ATP]) = 10^{7.3/1.364} = 2.25 \times 10^5$
(c) K_{eq} for $([B]_{eq} \times [ADP]_{eq} \times [P_i]_{eq} / [A]_{eq} [ATP]_{eq}) = 10^{3.3/1.364} = 263$

15

In this example, the hydrolysis of ATP changes the K_{eq} of conversion of A into B by a factor of 2.25 x 10^5 (263/0.00117). Typically the hydrolysis of ATP in a coupled reaction (or sequence of reactions) changes the equilibrium ratio of product to reactants by a factor of 10^{8n}, in which n is the number of ATP molecules involved in the overall reaction. Thus, the hydrolysis of 3 molecules of ATP generated during the respiratory oxidation of NADH can change the equilibrium constant of coupled reactions by a factor of 10^{24}. It must be emphasized, however, that this effect of ATP is not restricted to the levels of substrates and products in a chemical reaction but also applies to conformational changes between different proteins or to the movement of ions and molecules across membranes.

In the anaerobic glycolytic pathway, for example, the 12 kcal released in the complete oxidation of glyceraldehyde 3-phosphate to 3-phpsphogyceric acid would be lost if this reaction were not coupled to the formation of an "energy reach" acyl intermediate (acetyl-CoA). The energy trapped in this compound is then utilized in the endergonic process of ATP synthesis from ADP and P_i.

The transport of ions and metabolites is generally made through channels and pumps. Because a lipid bilayer is fundamentally impermeable to ions and metabolites, the transport of ions and metabolites across energy transducing membranes is assisted by *allosteric proteins* that behave in an enzyme-like manner. *Channels or pores* are *passive or facilitated diffusion devices* that allow metabolites to flow *spontaneously* in either way driven by a gradient of concentrations. *Active transport* systems of charged species require in addition the free energy of an electrical potential across the membrane. Whether a transport process is *passive* or *active* depend on the change in free energy of the transported species. For uncharged molecules the ΔG for the transport of species from side 1 where it is present at a concentration of c_1 to side 2 where it is present at concentration c_2 is

$$\Delta G = RT \, log_e \, c_2/c_1 = 2.303 \, RT \, log_{10} \, c_2/c_1 \qquad (4)$$

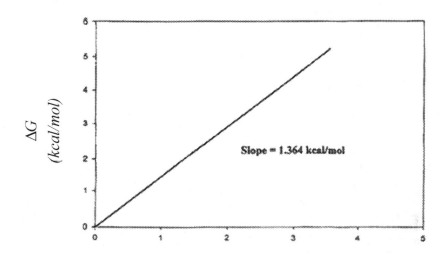

Figure II-1. The ΔG for passive transport systems depends on the concentration gradient of uncharged species [After Stryer *Biochemistry* (1995):309]

For charged species, the electrochemical potential, i.e. the sum of electrical ($nF\Delta\Psi$) and chemical concentration (c_2/c_1) terms, must be considered. The free energy change is then given by

$$\Delta G = 2.303 \; RT \log c_2/c_1 + nF\Delta\Psi \tag{5}$$

In which n is the electrical charge of the transported species, F is the Faraday (23.063 kcal V^{-1} mol $^{-1}$) and $\Delta\Psi$ is the membrane potential in volts across the membrane.

$$\Delta G = 1.364 \text{ kcal mole}^{-1} / 23.062 \text{ kcal } V^{-1} \text{ mole}^{-1}) = 0.059 \text{ volt} \tag{6}$$

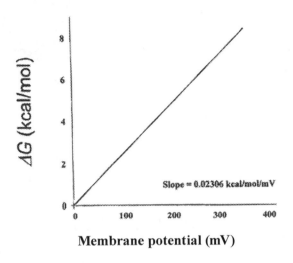

Figure II-2. The transport of charged molecules requires the ΔG of electrochemical potentials [After Stryer *Biochemistry* (1995):309]

Whether a transport process is passive or active depends on the change in free energy of the transported species. Consider, for example, a reaction in which the K'_{eq} is 1.0 and the concentration of a metabolite is 10^{-4} mM at side 1 and 10^{-2} mM at side 2 ($[c_2] \gg [c_1]$). The transference of this metabolite form side 1 to side 2 at 298° K will not occur because the ΔG is positive.

$$\Delta G = 2.303 \ RT \log 10^{-2} / 0^{-4}$$
$$\Delta G = 2.303 \times 1.987 \times 298 \times 2$$
$$\Delta G = 1.3637 \ \text{kcal/mol} \times 2 = +2.7 \ \text{kcal/moles}$$

Only when the concentration of a metabolite at side 1 is higher than at side 2 (see equation 6), i.e. when $[c_2] \ll [c_1]$ and both the ΔG and the term 2.303 $RT \log c_2/c_1$ are negative the process can take place.

An active transport requires a coupled input of free energy, whereas a passive transport system with a negative ΔG can occur spontaneously. *Whether a transport process is passive or active, i.e. takes place through channels of pumps, the extent of the transported species depends on the change in free energy of the transported species.*

Active transport systems that are carried out by *pumps* differ in essential ways from passive transport systems that are carried out by channels. An input of free energy is always required by the *pumps* to maintain the following essential functions of the cell. 1) Maintain the *steady-state* concentration of essential nutrients and metabolites in the face of wide fluctuations in the composition of the external environment. 2) Regulate the excitation and relaxation of muscle tissues and the transmission of information by the nervous systems, and 3) Control the volume of the cell by maintaining the osmotic pressure between compartments. The degree of selectivity of the pore depends on the diameter of the narrowest part of the pore. *Channels* (passive transport devises) formed from four subunits, such as the potassium and sodium channels, have the smallest pore diameter (3 and 5 A°, respectively) and are the most selective. Channels formed from six subunits, have a minimum diameter of about 16 A° and are the least selective.

Even when the ΔG of an *isolated* reaction is positive, the free energy coming from a *coupled* reaction with a large negative ΔG, such as the hydrolysis of ATP, will allow the pump to transfer a metabolite against a large concentration gradient. Thus the entrance of Na^+ and Ca^{2+} into the cell and the exit of K^+ can only occur when there is an extra input of free energy. Another example of active transport is the ejection of 1 Na^+ coupled to the uptake of 2 K^+, a process that only occurs when the reaction is sustained by the input of an *electrochemical potential*, i.e. when the contribution of the chemical (c_2/c_1 ratio) and electrical ($nF\Delta\Psi$) components result in overall negative ΔG.

The active transport of ions and metabolites depends on the redox potential. The $nF\Delta\Psi$ term in equation (6) is analogous to the $nF\Delta E_o$ term in oxidation-reduction reactions, in which the tendency of the *overall* oxidation-reduction reaction to go may be calculated from the difference between the reduction potential of the component half-reactions:

$$\Delta E_0 = [\Delta E_0 \text{ of the half reaction containing the oxidizing agent}]$$
$$- [\Delta E_0 \text{ of the half-reaction containing the reducing agent}] \quad (8)$$

If the oxidizing and reducing agents are identified correctly, the equation 8 always yields a positive ΔE_0. The values of E_0 represent electron pressure and, as such, they are independent of the number of electrons in the half-reaction. The ΔG of the reaction in terms of ΔE_0 can be calculated from the following relationship:

$$\Delta G = - nF\Delta E_0'. \quad (9)$$

The numerical value of oxidation-reduction reactions, $\Delta E_0'$, reflect the reduction potential relative to $2H^+ + 2e^- = H_2$ half reaction which is taken as -0.414 volt at pH 7.0 (see Table 1 (II-3). The value for the hydrogen half-reaction at pH 7.0 was calculated from the arbitrarily assigned value (ΔE_0) of 0.00 volt under true standard-state conditions of 1 M H^+ and 1 atmosphere H_2. For those few half-reactions of biological importance that do not involve H^+ as reactant, the E_0 and ΔE_0 values are essentially identical.

The free energy change imposed by a singly charged ion at 298 °K (23 °C) is related to the membrane potential by a straight line that has a slope equal to 0.023 kcal mV^{-1} $mole^{-1}$ (Fig. II-2)

In biological reactions the best oxidizing agent is the substrate which has the greater tendency to become reduced. If the oxidizing and reducing agents are identified correctly, equation (6) always yields a positive ΔE_0. The standard redox potential, E_0', may be considered as electron pressures and, as such, it is independent of the number of electrons in the half reaction. Because the membrane potential, E_m, is negative on the matrix side and positive on the cytosolic side of inner-mitochondrial membrane, the outer side of this membrane is known as the cytosolic or P side and the inner side as the matrix or N side.

Table II-1. The $\Delta E_o^{'}$ of half reactions involved in energy metabolism

Half-Reaction (Reductions at pH 7.0)	$\Delta E_o^{'}$ (volts)
$\frac{1}{2} O_2 + 2H^+ + 2e^- = H_2O$	0.816
$Fe^{+3} + 1e^- = Fe^{+2}$	0.771
Cytohrome $a_3 Fe^{+3} + 1e^- =$ cytohrome $a_3 Fe^{+2}$	0.55
$\frac{1}{2} O_2 + H_2O + 2e^- = H_2O_2$	0.30
Cytochrome $a Fe^{+3} + 1e^- =$ cytochrome $a Fe^{+2}$	0.29
Cytochrome $c Fe^{+3} + 1e^- =$ cytochrome $c Fe^{+2}$	0.29
Ubiquinone $+ 2H^+ + 2e^- =$ ubiquinone-H_2	0.10
Fumarate $+ 2H^+ + 2e^- =$ succinate	0.03
Pyruvate $+ NH_3 + 2H^+ + 2e^- =$ alanine	-0.13
α–Ketoglutarate $+ NH_3 + 2H^+ + 2e^- =$ Glutamate $+ H_2O$	-0.14
Oxalacetate $+ 2H^+ + 2e^- =$ malate	-0.175
$FAD + 2H^+ + 2e^- = FADH_2$	-0.18
Pyruvate $+ 2H^+ + 2e^- =$ lactate	-0.19
$NAD^+ + 2H^+ + 2e^- = NADH + H^+$	-0.32
$NADP^+ + 2H^+ + 2e^- = NADPH + H^+$	-0.32
Pyruvate $+ CO_2 + 2H^+ + 2e^- =$ malate	-0.33
$2H^+ + 2e^- = H_2$	-0.414
Succinate $+ CO_2 + 2H^+ + 2e^- = \alpha$–Ketoglutarate $+ H_2O$	-0.67

II. 3. Most important forms of metabolic energy

Metabolism is the complex of physical and chemical processes occurring within a living cell or organism that are necessary for the maintenance of life. During metabolism some substances are broken down to yield energy for vital processes while other substances, necessary for life, are synthesized. The amount of energy liberated during the catabolism or breakdown of foodstuff is the same as the amount liberated when food is burned outside the body.

The type, extent and rates of free energy directly involved in the metabolic process of aerobic organisms depend on the accessibility of respiratory substrates, the amount of enzymes and their catalytic activity. An important general principle in the regulation of metabolic energy is that the *synthesis and degradation of reactants are almost always distinct*, and take place in different compartments of the cell. Thus, fatty acid oxidation occurs in mitochondria, whereas fatty acid synthesis occurs in the cytosol. Also, the *endergonic and sigmoidal process of ATP synthesis takes place in the mitochondrial matrix* and depends on both the concentrations of oxygen and ADP. Distinctly, the *exergonic and hyperbolical process of ATP hydrolysis takes place outside the mitochondria* and depends on the concentration of ATP and the metabolic activity of the cell. Regulation and flexibility of metabolic energy is also observed in reactions in which a biosynthetic pathway is allosterically controlled by the ultimate product of the pathway. Although the aerobic process of oxygen reduction to water is apparently simple, the generation and utilization of the free energy involved in the oxidative phosphorylation process of ATP synthesis is extremely complex. Most of the electrons utilized in the liberation of free energy come from the oxidation of NADH and $FADH_2$, the metabolites from glycolysis and the tri-carboxylic acid cycle (TCA).

Energy charge and phosphorylation potential—Because the *energy status* of the cell is controlled by the concentrations of ATP, ADP, and AMP, Atkinson considered that the *relative* concentration o these substances represent the *energy charge of the cell*. Furthermore, since ATP contains two anhydride bonds, ADP contains one, and AMP is formed during the pyrophosphate cleavage of ATP, the energy charge of the cell was defined by the following relation.

$$\text{Energy charge} = \frac{[ATP] + [ADP]}{[ATP] + [ADP] + [AMP]}$$

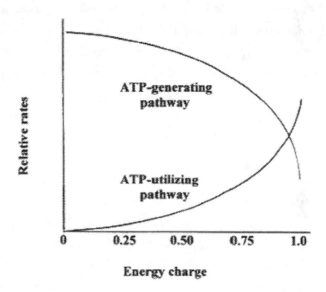

Figure II-3. Effect of the energy charge of the cell on the relative rates of typical catabolic (ATP generating) and anabolic (ATP utilizing) reactions

The value of the *energy charge* ranges from 0 (all nucleotide in the form of AMP) to 1.0 (all nucleotides in the form of ATP). During catabolism, i.e. the breakdown of complex molecules, the ATP-generating pathway is inhibited as the energy charge of the cell increases. On the contrary, during anabolic reactions in which complex molecules are formed from simple molecules, the relative rates of ATP synthesis increase as the energy charge increases. In accordance with these principles, the rates of both O_2 uptake and ATP synthesis are *minimal* when the energy-charge is *maximal*, i.e. when the mitochondrial membrane is saturated with O_2 and ATP. On the contrary, when the energy-charge of the cell is *minimal* and the concentrations of O_2 and ATP are *extremely low* the rates of O_2 consumption and ATP synthesis become *maximal* the instant in which O_2 is made available. When catabolic and anabolic processes are equal the energy charge of the cell, like the pH, is buffered and maintained between the narrow limits of 0.8 and 0.95.

An alternative index of the energy status of the cell is the *phosphorylation potential, ΔGp*, which is represented by the following equation:

$$\Delta Gp = \Delta G^{o'} + RT \ln [ATP] / [ADP] [P_i]$$

The phosphorylation potential, in contrast with the energy charge, depends on the concentration of P_i and is directly related to the free energy available from ATP. These two forms of energy are a daily occurrence in aerobic organisms. Thus, after abrupt physical exercises, when both the *levels of O_2 and the energy charge of the cell have greatly decreased*, the ensuing rates of O_2 consumption and ATP synthesis may attain maximal values as soon O_2 diffuses from cytosol to matrix. Under absolute resting conditions (profound sleep for example), when the concentration of O_2 inside the mitochondria is maximal, the *rates of O_2 consumption and ATP synthesis are minimal* but the energy charge of the cell is *maximal*. Depending on the degree of activity of the cell the actual concentrations of O_2 inside the mitochondria varies from near zero to a maximum of about 66 μM. The concentrations of ATP, ADP and AMP are given in Table II-2.

Table II-2. The adenine nucleotide content of some tissues
[After A. Lehninger *Biochemistry* (1975):539]

	ATP	ADP	AMP
Guinea pig brain	2.98	0.7	0.13
Rat heart	13.3	2.6	0.43
Blowfly muscle	14.0	3.0	0.25

Metabolic rate (MR)—In humans the *metabolic rate* is defined as the amount of energy liberated per unit of time. This form of energy is utilized in the performance of external work, the storage of useful forms of energy and the maintenance of temperature,

Energy output = External work + Energy storage + Heat

The efficiency of metabolic energy is defined by the following relationship

Efficiency = Work done / Total energy expended

During isometric muscle contraction, for example, most of the energy liberated appears as heat, because little or no external work (the force multiplied by the distanced that the force moves a mass) is done. In fact, any energy generated by the cell that is not utilized is stored in energy-reach compounds, fundamentally in the form of ATP. Under absolute resting conditions, essentially all of the energy output appears as heat. Energy production can also be evaluated by measuring the extent of O_2 consumption in what is called indirect calorimetry. Because O_2 is not stored and since the amount of O_2 consumed per unit time is proportionate to the energy liberated, the amount of energy released per mole of O_2 consumed varies slightly with the type of compound being oxidized. The approximate energy liberation per liter of O_2 consumed is 4.82 kcal, and for many purposes this value is accurate enough. In humans, the *metabolic rate* is affected by a multitude of factors amongst which the most important are muscular exercise, recent ingestion of food, high or low environmental temperature, emotional state, circulating levels of thyroid hormones, epinephrine and norepinephrine, sex, age height, weight, and surface area.

Basal metabolic rate (BMR)—In general the *basal metabolic rate* is defined as the number of calories released by an organism at complete rest per kilogram of body weight or square meter of body surface per hour. In humans, the basal metabolic rate is determined under a set of widely known and accepted standard conditions (resting state, room temperature, 12-14 hours after the last meal, etc.). The BMR of a man of average size is about 2000 kcal per hour and m^2 of surface. In females, the BMR at all ages is slightly lower than in males. The BMR is also higher in children and declines with age. An increase in body temperature speeds up chemical reaction, and the BMR rises approximately 14% for each Celsius degree of fever. The metabolic rate is not truly "basal" because the metabolic rate during sleep is lower than the "basal".

The relationship between surface body area (S) in m^2, weight (W) in Kg, and height (H) in cm can be expressed by the following formula:

$$S = 0.007184 \times W^{0.425} \times H^{0.725}$$

The slope of the line that relates metabolic rate and *surface body area* equal to 0.67 is more precise than the line that relates metabolic rate and body weight. The *basal metabolic rate* (BMR) of a man of average size is about 2000 kcal/d. Large animals have higher absolute basal metabolic rates, but the ratio of BMR to body weight in small animal is much greater.

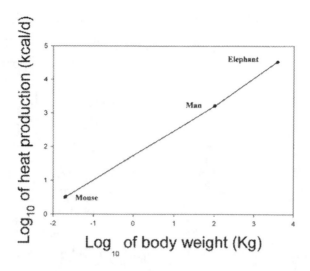

Figure II-4. The extent of heat production in kcal/ day increases exponentially depending on *body weight* [Modified from W. F.Ganong (1993) *Physiology* (1993):256].

Specific dynamic action (SDA)—The metabolic rate is affected by many factors (muscular exercise, ingestion of foods, environmental temperature, body weight, sex, age, emotional state, circulating levels of epinephrine, norepinephrine and thyroid hormones). The SDA of a food is the obligatory energy expenditure that occurs during its assimilation into the body. An amount of protein sufficient to provide 100 kcal increases the metabolic rate 30 kcal; a similar amount of carbohydrate increases it 6 kcal; and a similar amount of fat, 4 kcal. This difference indicates that the energy used in their assimilation must come from the food itself or from the body energy stores. The cause for the specific dynamic action, which may last up to 6 hours, is not known.

Respiratory quotient, RQ, is the ratio at *steady state* between the volume of CO_2 produced and O_2 consumed per unit of time. Because in carbohydrates the amount of H and O are present in the same proportion as in water (twice as much H than O), the RQ of carbohydrates is exactly 1.00. In fats, on the other hand, the RQ is only 0.703 because an extra amount of O_2 is necessary for the formation of H_2O. The average RQ of proteins has been calculated to be close 0.82.

II. 4. Electrons enter the mitochondria via specific shuttles

Because the inner mitochondrial membrane is for the most part impermeable to ions and metabolites, a large fraction of the free energy released during the respiratory process of electron flow is used for the transport of ions and metabolites. In the process of oxidative phosphorylation, for example, the protein in charge to transport the highly charged molecules of ADP and ATP is called *ADP-ATP translocase or adenine nucleotide carrier*. The *phosphate carrier* that transports the single charged P_i^- anion in concert with the *adenine nucleotide carrier* mediates either the anti-port of P_i^- for H^+ or the electro neutral sym-port of P_i^- and H^+.

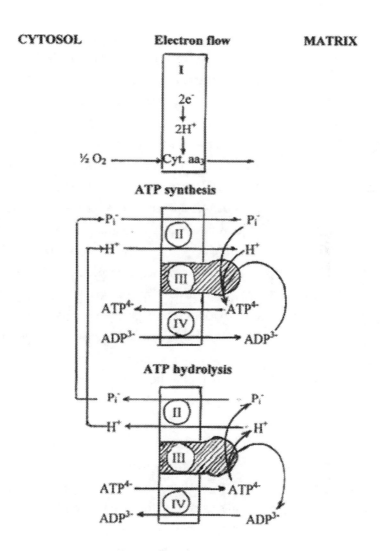

Figure II-5. Transport of electrons H⁺, Pᵢ, ADP and ATP across the membrane (I = respiratory chain, II = phosphate translocase, III = ATP synthase, IV = ATP-ADP translocase).

The *ADP-ATP translocase* specifically transports ADP, ATP, dADP, and dATP but not AMP or other closely related nucleotides such as GTP, GDP, CTP, and CDP. The *adenine nucleotide translocase*

---

contains a *single* nucleotide binding site that allows the entrance of ADP or ATP (devoid of Mg^{2+}) with the same affinity. The rate of the binding-site eversion from the matrix to the cytosolic side of the membrane is nearly 30 times faster for the exit of ATP than for the entrance of ADP because, in the presence of a positive membrane potential, ATP is more negatively charged than ADP. The translocase does not evert at an appreciable rate unless a nucleotide is bound, thus guarantying that the entry of ADP into the matrix is precisely coupled to the exit of ATP. The translocase, and the entire process of oxidative phosphorylation, is inhibited by the plant glycoside atractyloside on the cytosolic side of the membrane and by the antibiotic bonkrekic acid on its matrix side. The process of ATP synthesis immediately stops in the presence of these inhibitors, indicating that the ADP-ATP translocase is essential for the process of oxidative phosphorylation that takes place in intact mitochondria. Obviously, these inhibitors have absolutely no effect on the process of ATP synthesis that is catalyzed by inverted inner-membrane vesicles in which the ATP-synthase is directly exposed to its substrates, and neither ADP nor P_i have the need to be translocated.

The phosphoryl potential of ATP (a free-energy change derived from position or condition motion) depends on two factors: the electrostatic repulsion and resonance stabilization. At pH 7.0 the triphosphate unit of ATP carries about four negative charges. These charges repel one another strongly because they are in close proximity. In ADP the repulsion between them is reduced because they enjoy greater resonance stabilization than in ATP.

Reactions with positive ΔG values cannot occur unless they are coupled to a reaction with a higher negative ΔG value like those associated with the hydrolysis of ATP. The transfer of H^+, Na^+, Ca^{2+}, P_i, and ADP across the inner mitochondrial membrane would not occur in the absence of the hydrolysis of ATP. Various other compounds in biological systems have a high phosphoryl potential

Table II-3. Free energy of hydrolysis of some
phosphorylated compounds

Compound	$\Delta G^{o'}$ (kcal/mol)
Phosphoenolpyruvate	-14.8
Carbamoyl phosphate	-12.4
Acetyl phosphate	-10.3
Creatine phosphate	-10.3
Pyrophosphate	-8.0
ATP hydrolysis to ADP	-7.3
Glucose-1-phosphate	-5.0
Glucose-6-phosphate	-3.3
Glucose-3-phosphate	-2.2

More than one third of the ATP consumed by a resting animal is used for the transport of essential ions and metabolites, which like Ca^{2+} are key intracellular messengers in many eukaryotic signal transduction processes

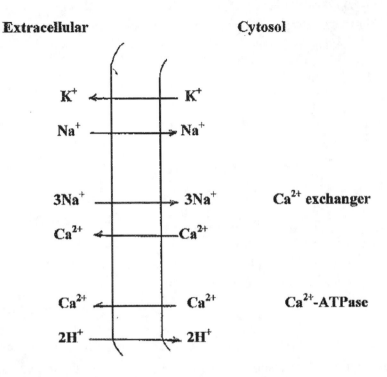

Figure II-6. Transport of H^+, Ca^{2+} Na^+ and K^+ across the plasma membrane

The large electrochemical gradient of Ca^{2+} that exists across the plasma membrane is maintained by: a) an ATP-driven calcium pump called *Ca^{2+}-ATPase* and b) a *sodium-calcium exchanger* that uses the Na^+ gradient across the plasma membrane.

"The calcium level in many intracellular compartments is much higher than in the cytosol. The *endoplasmic reticulum* (ER), an extensive membrane-enclosed network, serves as a large and readily mobilized internal source of Ca^{2+}. The *Ca^{2+}-ATPase* in the ER membrane *pumps* Ca^{2+} into this compartment. A cycle of conformational changes occur when two Ca^{2+} ions are transported across the *sarcoplasmic reticulum pump* of muscles driven by the hydrolysis of ATP in a process that is similar to that occurring in the

Na^+- K^+ ATPase cycle. Under all physiological conditions, the influx of Ca^{2+} is thermodynamically favorable because the cytosolic Ca^{2+} level of an unexcited cell is close to 0.1 µM compared with an extracellular concentration.

The influx of Ca^{2+} is thermodynamically favorable under all physiological conditions. The cytosolic Ca^{2+} level of an unexcited cell is close to 0.1 µM compared with an extracellular concentration of 1.5 mM. Under typical cellular conditions, the entry of Na^+ provides a free energy input of 2.2 kcal per mol (117 mM outside and 30 mM inside and a membrane potential of -56 mV). This membrane potential is sufficient to generate a 36.7-fold concentration gradient of an uncharged molecule such as glucose. Many actively transported processes are not *directly* driven by the hydrolysis of ATP. Instead, the uphill flow of an ion or molecules is coupled to the downhill flow of another ion. Thus, the sodium gradient across the plasma membrane can be trapped to drive the entrance as well as the extrusion of molecules. The sodium-calcium exchanger in the plasma membrane uses the electrochemical gradient of Na^+ to pump Ca^{2+} out of the cell. Three Na^+ ions enter the cell for each Ca^{2+} that is extruded. The cost of transport by this exchanger is paid by the Na^+-K^+ *pump*, which generates the requisite sodium gradient. The exchanger has *lower affinity for Ca^{2+} than thus the Ca^{2+}-ATPase, but its capacity to extrude Ca^{2+} is greater.*

In exchanger-pumps, the binding site for transported species is not simultaneously accessible from both sides of the membrane as it is in an *open pore or channel* where an ion can flow at any instant from either side. The direction of ion movement is only determined by the electrochemical gradient. Distinctly, in active transport the eversion of the site is coupled to a phosphorylation-dephosphorylation cycle or to the binding and transport of another ion. The sodium gradient across the plasma membrane can be trapped to drive the entry as well as the extrusion of molecules. Under typical cellular conditions (117 mM external and 30 mM internal) the entry of Na^+

provides a membrane potential of -56 mV, which is enough to generate a 36.7-fold gradient of an uncharged molecules such as glucose. The antiporter NHE_1 that transports Na^+ and H^+ in opposite directions is implicated in some cardiovascular diseases in processes regulated by the Ca^{2+}-binding protein calmodulin (CaM), The Ca^{2+} exchanger can extrude about 2000 ions per second, compared with only 30 per second for the Ca^{2+}-ATPase pump. However, both of these rates are orders of magnitude slower than the rates of translocation through channels, which are $\sim 10^7$ per second. In general, transport systems that require an input of energy are much slower than those through channels.

The inner mitochondrial membrane is impermeable to NAD^+, NADH, $NADP^+$, NADPH, AMP, CTP, GTP, CDP, GDP, CoA, acetyl-CoA, and a poll of fuel molecules such as glucose, amino acids and fatty acids. The cytosolic pool of these molecules enters the mitochondrial matrix via specific routes or shuttles where they are structurally transformed before entering the respiratory chain.

The passage of solutes such as inorganic phosphate, ATP, ADP, citrate, glycerol 3-phosphate, α-ketoglutarate and aspartate take place through specific membrane-transport systems or channels. Thus, in the *glycerol 3-phosphate shuttle* (see Fig. II -6) the *cytosolic* glycerol 3-phosphate *dehydrogenase* (E_1) catalyzes first the reduction of dihydroxyacetone phosphate (DHAP) with H^+ and NADH forming NAD^+ and glycerol 3-phosphate (G 3-P) that than *diffuses into the mitochondria*. Glycerol 3-phosphate is reoxidized to DHAP on the outer phase of the membrane, where a pair of electrons from G 3-P are transferred to the FAD prosthetic group of the *transmembrane* glycerol-3 phosphate dehydrogenase (E_2). This enzyme differs from the cytosolic counterpart because is a transmembrane protein and uses FAD rather than NAD^+ as the electron acceptor. The DHAP formed in the mitochondrial membrane *diffuses* back into the cytosol to complete the shuttle.

CYTOSOL

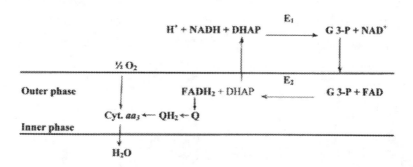

Figure II-7. Transfer of electrons from cytosolic NADH to respiratory chain *via* the *glycerol 3-phosphate shuttle*.

The reduced flavin, $FADH_2$, inside the mitochondria transfers its electrons to `the electron cattier Q, which then enters the respiratory chain as QH_2 to transfer electrons to cytochrome aa_3 where the incoming O_2 is reduced to water. The use of FAD enables electrons contained in cytosolic NADH to be transported to the mitochondrial matrix *against a NADH concentration gradient*. The difference in the redox potential ($\Delta E^{o'}$) that occur during the oxidation of NADH coming from the citric acid cycle (1.136 volts) is higher than the $\Delta E^{o'}$ that occur during the oxidation of $FADH_2$ (0.996 volts). Consequently, the extent of ATP formed is 12.3% lower in the presence of $FADH_2$ than in the presence of NADH. The high-potential electrons contained in NADH and $FADH_2$ are then transferred to the respiratory chain where O_2 is reduced to water.

In heart and liver, electrons from cytosolic NADH are brought into mitochondria by the *malate-aspartate shuttle*, which is mediated by two membrane carriers and 4 enzymes. Electrons from NADH reduce oxaloacetate to malate by the *cytosolic malate dehydrogenase* (E_1). Malate enters the matrix where is oxidized by the *mitochondrial malate dehydrogenase* (E_2) to regenerate NADH and oxaloacetate.

Electrons from NADH enter the respiratory chain to reduce O_2 to water at the level of the cytochrome oxidase (E_5). The oxaloacetate-aspartate transaminase (E_3) at the matrix side of the mitochondria transforms oxaloacetate into aspartate that returns to the cytosolic side to be desaminated to oxaloacetate by the oxaloacetate-aspartate transaminase (E_4).

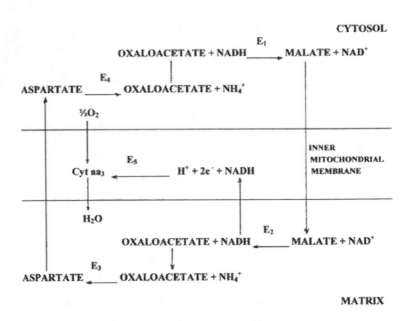

Figure II-8. Transfer of electrons from cytosolic NADH to the respiratory chain *via malate-aspartate shuttle*.

II. 5. Acetyl CoA is the common entrance of electrons to the Krebs cycle

Electrons and protons contained in fuel molecules such as glucose, amino acids and fatty acids enter the citric or Krebs cycle via the energy-charged molecule of acetyl-CoA (see Fig. II-9). The Krebs cycle is the common pathway for the final oxidation of fuel molecules at the matrix side of the mitochondria. These molecules are first dehydrogenated by flavin-linked dehydrogenases to form 3 molecules of NADH, one molecule of $FADH_2$, and 2 of CO_2. The high-potential electrons contained in NADH and $FADH_2$ are then directly transferred to the respiratory chain where O_2 is reduced to water. The oxidative decarboxilation of pyruvate to form acetyl CoA, *which occurs in the mitochondrial matrix*, is the link between the citric acid cycle and the oxidation of glucose, fatty acids, and amino acids. The sequences of reactions that take place in the entire *Krebs cycle* are depicted in figures II-9 and the related Tables II-4 and II-5.

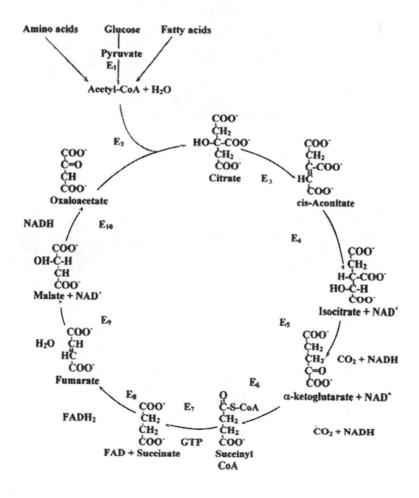

The 10 enzymes involved in the catalysis of these reactions and the standard free energy changes ($\Delta G^{o'}$) that occur in the Krebs cycle are shown in Table II-5.

Table II-4. The 10 enzymatically catalyzed reactions
of the Krebs cycle

E_1	Pyruvate dehydrogenase complex
E_2	Citrate synthase
E_3	cis-Aconitase
E_4	Aconitase
E_5	Isocitrate dehydrogenase
E_6	α-ketoglutarate dehydrogenase
E_7	Succinyl CoA synthase
E_8	Succinate dehydrogenase
E_9	Fumarase
E_{10}	Malate dehydrogenase

The overall decarboxilation of pyruvate, the formation of acetyl CoA and the reduction of NAD^+ to NADH, that are the main sources of electrons for the respiratory chain, are represented by the following deceivingly simple reaction.

$$Pyruvate + CoA + NAD^+ = acetyl\ CoA + CO_2 + NADH$$

The irreversible funneling of pyruvate into the mitochondrial matrix takes place in five consecutive steps catalyzed by a multimeric assembly of three kinds of enzymes that in conjunction constitute the *pyruvate dehydrogenase complex* (Tables II-5 and II-6).

Table II-5. Enzymes and prosthetic groups in the pyruvate
dehydrogenase complex

Enzyme	Prosthetic group	Type of reaction
Pyruvate dehydrogenase (E_1)	TPP	Oxidative decarboxilation of pyruvate
Dihydrolipoyl transacetylase (E_2)	Lipoamide	Transfer of the acetyl group to CoA
Dihydrolipoyl dehydrogenase (E_3)	FAD	Regeneration of the oxidized form of lipoamide

Table II-6. Standard free energy change, $\Delta G^{o'}$,
for the reaction of the Krebs cycle

Reactions	Enzyme	Type of reaction	$\Delta G^{o'}$
Acetyl CoA + oxaloacetate to citrate + CoA	Citrate synthase (2)	Condensation	-7.5
Citrate to *cis* aconitate	Aconitase (3)	Dehydration	+2.0
cis aconitate to isocitrate	Aconitase (4)	Hydration	-0.5
Isocitratrate to α-ketoglutarate	Isocitrate dehydrogenase (5)	Dehydration and oxidation	-2.0
α-ketoglutarate to succinyl CoA	α-ketoglutarate-dehydrogenease complex (6)	Dehydration and oxidation	-7.2
Succinyl CoA to succinate	Succinyl CoA synthase (7)	Substrate-level phosphorylation	-0.8
Succinate to fumarate	Succinate dehydrogenase (8)	Oxidation	0.0
Fumarate to L-malate	Fumarase (9)	Hydration	-0.9
L-malate to oxaloacetate	Malate dehydrogenase (10)	Oxidation	+7.1

Remember that a reaction can only occur spontaneously when ΔG is negative. A negative ΔG means that the reaction as written will proceed from left to right towards a state of equilibrium. A positive $\Delta G^{o'}$ indicates that the reaction will proceed only if there is an input of free energy. Since the large number of reactions that occur in the cycle take place with negative than positive $\Delta G^{o'}$ (-18.9 versus +9.1 kcal/mole), it is evident that the cycle can spontaneously proceed until equilibrium is attained.

In the first phase of the reaction, catalyzed by pyruvate dehydrogenase (E_1), pyruvate is decarboxylated by combining with thiamine pyrophosphate (TPP), the prosthetic group of pyruvate dehydrogenase, thus forming hydroxyethyl-TPP and CoA.

$$\text{Pyruvate} + \text{TPP} \_\_\_\_ E_1 _____ \text{hydroxyethyl-TPP} + \text{CoA}$$

The hydroxyethyl group attached to TPP is then oxidized to form an acetyl group and concomitantly transferred to *lipoamide* to form acetyllipoamide.

$$\text{Hydroxyethyl-TPP} + \text{Lipoamide} \_ E_2 \_ \text{Carbonion of TPP} + \\ \text{Acetyllipoamide}$$

In the second phase of the reaction the acetyl group is transferred from *acetyllipoamide to CoA*, in a reaction catalyzed by *dihydrolipoyl transacetylase* (E_2).

$$\text{Acetyllipoamide} + \text{HS-CoA} \_ E_2 \_ \text{Dihyrolipoamide} + \text{Acetil CoA}$$

The oxidized form of lipoamide is regenerated in two consecutive steps of a reaction catalyzed by dyhydrolipoyl dehydrogenase (E_3). In the first step, the prosthetic group of the enzyme, FAD, receives first 2 electrons that are then passed to NAD^+ to form NAD

Dihyrolipoamide + FAD _____ E_3_____ Lipoamide + FADH$_2$
FADH$_2$ + NAD$^+$ ___ E_3_____ NADH + FAD + H$^+$

Although the formation of pyruvate during the glycolytic reaction can occur *in the absence oxygen* the complete oxidation of pyruvate in the *Krebs cycle, which takes place on the matrix side of mitochondria, cannot operate in the absence oxygen*. The reason is that the oxidation of isocitrate to α-ketoglutarate cannot takes place in the absence of NAD$^+$, which is formed during the glycolytic process in which pyruvate is reduced to lactate.

The 5 enzymatic reactions involved in the complete transfer of electrons from pyruvate to oxygen are presented in Fig. II-10.

E_1
A + B ---- C + C$_o$A   **Step I**
$\downarrow$ E_2
C + D ---- B + E   **Step II**
$\downarrow$ E_3
E + F ---- G + H   **Step III**
$\downarrow$ E_3
G + I ---- D + J   **Step IV**
$\downarrow$ R.C.
J + K ---- I + L ---- O$_2$ **Step V**

In this figure, the 5 the steps in the transfer of electrons from pyruvate to O$_2$ are represented by: A = pyruvate, B = TPP or thiamine pyrophosphate, C = hydroxyl ethyl pyrophosphate, D = lipoamide, E = acetyllipoamide, F = CoA-SH, G = dihydrolipoamide, H = acetyl CoA, I = FAD, J = FADH$_2$, K = NAD$^+$ and L = NADH. The final step V is the transfer of electrons from NADH to O$_2$ by the respiratory chain (R.C.)

KINETICS OF ENZYME CATALYZED REACTIONS

III. 1. Introduction

Enzymes are molecular devises that enhance the rates of chemical reactions several orders of magnitude without affecting the state of equilibrium during which the rates of the forward and reverse reactions are exactly the same. The first step in catalysis is the binding of a substrate to an active-cleft from which water is largely excluded during the formation of the ES complex. The most remarkable characteristics of these molecules are their catalytic power and specificity. The rates of catalyzed reactions can be up to 10 orders of magnitude higher than those occurring in the absence of enzymes. For example, the rate of hydration of CO_2, which is essential for the transfer of CO_2 from tissues to the alveolar air *via* the vascular system, is 10^5 per second, i.e. 10^7 faster than the rate of the uncatalyzed reaction. Enzymes select their *substrates* with a high degree of specificity. The most important factors in determining the rates of catalysis under *in vivo* conditions are the concentration of enzymes and substrates, the presence of specific regulators (activators or inhibitors), the temperature, the pH and the ionic strength of the medium.

III. 2. Kinetic orders and steady-state conditions

The general assumption is that the first step in catalysis is the formation of the enzyme-substrate complex (ES) which forms and dissociates with characteristic rate constants (see Figs. III-1 & III-2).

$$E + S \underset{k2}{\overset{k1}{\rightleftharpoons}} ES \underset{k4}{\overset{k3}{\rightleftharpoons}} E + P$$

In the *forward* direction the ES complex is formed with a rate constant, k_1, and dissociates into free enzyme E and product P with another rate constant, k_3. In the *reverse* direction the ES complex dissociates into free enzyme and substrate with the rate constant k_2. In the majority of biological reactions the reverse formation of the ES complex from product and free enzyme is negligible and the rate constant k_4 in equation 1 is close to zero (Fig. III-2)

$$E + S \underset{k_2}{\overset{k_1}{\rightleftharpoons}} ES \overset{k_3}{\longrightarrow} E + P$$

The overall velocity of the reaction depends on the difference between the rate of formation and the rate of breakdown of ES

Rate of formation of ES $= k_1$ [E] [S]
Rate of breakdown of ES $= (k_2 + k_3)$ [ES]

Even when k_4 is zero, the *maximal velocity* of the reaction depends on a multitude of factors. In the respiratory process of O_2 reduction to water, for example, the concentration of ES depends on the degree of reduction of the cytochrome aa_3, the ionic strength of the medium, and the relative concentrations of electrons, protons and oxygen.

Maximal rates of oxygen consumption are only attained when the cytochrome aa_3 is fully reduced and there is no excess of oxygen or *impairing oxygen radicals*.

Zero order reactions are those occurring in the presence of *saturating concentrations of all the substrates involved in the reaction* ([S] >> [E]) and *when the rates of reaction have attained maximal values,* V_{max}. Under these conditions the rates of reaction are independent of substrate concentration.

First order reactions are those which proceed at a rate exactly proportional to the concentration of one reactant. In reactions catalyzed by enzymes having a single catalytic site and the substrate concentration is much lower than the enzyme concentration ([S] << [E]), the rate of substrate utilization is represented by the following equation.

$$- d\,[S]\,/\,dt = k\,[S] \tag{3}$$

The integrated form of a reaction of first order is more useful for carrying out kinetic calculations,

$$\ln [S_o]\,/\,[S_t] = kt\,/2.303 \tag{4}$$

in which $[S_o]$ is the concentration of substrate at time zero and [S] the concentration at time t. Thus in reactions of first order the half-time, $t_{1/2}$, is independent of the *initial concentration of substrate* and the ln of 2 is 0.693.

$$t_{1/2} = 0.693\,/\,k \tag{5}$$

Thus the velocity v_o the reaction is the product of the concentration of the ES complex and the *specific reaction rate constant* k_3 which has the dimensions of reciprocal of time, usually s^{-1}.

$$V = k_3\,[ES] \tag{6}$$

Second order reactions are those in which the rate is proportional to *the product of concentrations of two reactants or the second power of a single reactant.* The rate of transformations of substrates (A and B or A^2) into product is given by

$$- d[A] / dt = k [A] [B] \qquad (7)$$
or
$$-d[A] / dt = k [A] [A] = k [A]^2$$

where *k is the second-order rate constant* that has the dimensions of M^{-1} s^{-1} or 1/ (concentration x time). The integrated form of the second-order rate equation is

$$t = 2.303 / k ([A_o] - [B_o]) \times \log [B_o] [A] / [A_o] [B] \qquad (8)$$

where $[A_o]$ and $[B_o]$ are initial concentrations and [A] and [B] are the concentrations at time *t*.

It is important to emphasize that a second-order reaction may under some conditions appear to be a *first-order* reaction. In the following respiratory process:

$$\tfrac{1}{2} O_2 + 2 H^+ + 2e^- = H_2O$$

Under absolute resting conditions, for example, the rates of respiration are close to zero-order in O_2 consumption because the rates of O_2 consumption do not depend on O_2 concentration. Distinctly, after an abrupt and strenuous physical exercise, when the level of O_2 has dropped to near anaerobiosis and the mitochondria are saturated with H^+ and electrons, the rates of O_2 consumption are first-order the instant in which O_2 diffuses from cytosol to matrix.

Third-order reactions are those whose velocity is proportional to the product of three concentration terms. However, reaction rates need not necessarily be pure first order or pure second order; frequently they are of mixed order

The *Steady state* of an enzyme catalyzed reaction is defined as a stable condition in which the rate of the overall reaction does not change over time or the rate of reaction in one direction is continually balanced by the rate of the reaction in opposite direction. This condition exists when at the beginning of the reaction the concentration of substrate is much higher than the concentration of enzyme ($[S] \gg [E]$) and the level of the ES complex remains constant for a prolonged period of time, i.e. when

$$d\,[E\,S]\,/\,dt = 0 \tag{9}$$

Under physiological conditions, however, the concentration of the ES complex remains constant only under exceptional conditions. During absolute resting conditions (profound sleep for example), the [ES] may remain unchanged for a long time only when the level of O_2 is in excess and the redox state of cytochrome aa_3 remains constant because the rates of entrance and exit of electrons to and from this enzyme are equal.

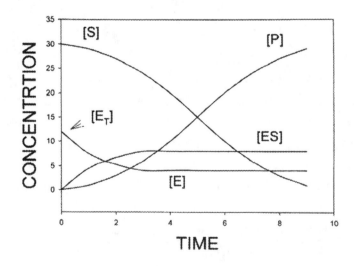

Figure III-3. Time-course of formation of the enzyme-substrate complex [After Lehninger, *Biochemistry* (1975) p. 190]

III. 3. The Michaelis-Menten constant of hyperbolical reactions

A distinctive feature of enzyme-catalyzed reactions, not generally observed in chemical reactions, is the phenomenon of substrate saturation. When an enzyme has a single catalytic site and the binding of its substrate has no effect on the dissociation constant of this site a plot of rates of reaction versus substrate concentration yield a *hyperbolical* curve. Even for enzymes with multiple catalytic-sites, when the binding of a substrate to one site has no structural or conformational effects on adjacent sites the velocity of the reaction depends *hyperbolically* on substrate concentration.

Under these conditions, the kinetic property of a large number of enzyme-catalyzed reactions, including the reduction of O_2 by the cytochrome oxidase and the *hydrolysis* of ATP at the level of the F_0F_1 ATP synthase, follow Michaelis-Menten kinetics. The model proposes that the ES complex, which is the most important intermediate in enzymatic reactions, breaks down in the forward direction to form free E and product or in the reverse direction to reform substrate and E. (see equation # 2).

When the rate of formation of ES is equal to its rate of breakdown,

$$k_1 [E] [S] = k_2 [ES] + k_3 [ES] \tag{10}$$
or
$$k_1 [E] [S] = (k_2 + k_3) [ES] \tag{11}$$
and
$$[E] [S] / [ES] = k_2 + k_3 / k_1 \tag{12}$$

the lump of rate constants that appear in equation 12 is called the Michaelis-Menten `constant or K_M.

$$K_M = (k_2 + k_3) / k_1 \tag{13}$$

The steady state concentration of the ES complex can be obtained by solving for [ES] in equation 12.

$$[ES] = [E] [S] / K_M \tag{14}$$

When the concentration of enzyme is much lower than that of the substrate and the concentration of free enzyme [E] is equal to the difference between the concentration of total enzyme (E_T) and ES complex, i.e. when

$$[E] = [E_T] - [ES] \tag{15}$$

the reaction in equation 14 becomes:

$$[ES] = ([E_T] - [ES]) \, [S] / \textbf{\textit{K}}_M \tag{16}$$
$$[ES] = [E_T] \, [S] / [S] + \textbf{\textit{K}}_M \tag{17}$$

Substituting [ES] for its value in equation 6:

$$V = k_3 \, [E_T] \, [S] / [S] + \textbf{\textit{K}}_M \tag{18}$$

The maximal rate, V_{max}, is attained when [S] is much greater than $\textbf{\textit{K}}_M$ and the catalytic sites on the enzyme are saturated with substrate. Under these conditions the term $[S] / [S] + \textbf{\textit{K}}_M$ in equation 18 is equal to 1.0 and

$$V_{max} = k_3 \, [E_T] \tag{19}$$

Now, replacing the value of V_{max} in equation 18 we obtain the Michaelis-Menten relationship between V and V_{max}

$$V = V_{max} \, [S] / [S] + \textbf{\textit{K}}_M \tag{20}$$

At very low substrate concentrations, when [S] is much smaller than the $\textbf{\textit{K}}_M$, the rate is directly proportional to substrate concentration (see figure III-2). The rate of reaction is independent of substrate concentration only in reactions of zero order when the substrate concentration is much greater than the $\textbf{\textit{K}}_M$. Although the

Michaelis-Menten constant (equation 13) has no term for substrate concentration, the meaning of K_M is contained in V_{max}:

$$K_M = [S] \qquad (21)$$

The K_M. of a reaction can only be calculated when maximal rates attained under true zero-order conditions are clearly evaluated.

$$1/V = K_M / V_{max} \times [S] + 1/V_{max} \qquad (22)$$

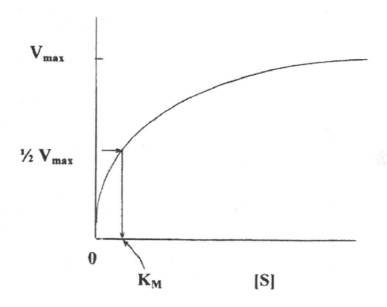

Figure III-4. *The K_M is equal to the substrate concentration at which the reaction rate (V) is half its maxima value (V_{max}).*

K_M values of some relevant enzymes is presented in Table III-1, including the most recently obtained K_M of isolated cytochrome oxidase for O_2, determined in the presence of *in vivo* levels of O_2 [Reynafarje & Ferreira, *J. Bioenerg. Biomembr.* (2002), 34, 259-267].

Table III-1. Comparative K_M values for some enzymes.

Enzyme	Substrate	K_M (μM)
Carbonic unhydrase	CO_2	8000
Chymotrypsin	Acetyl-$_L$-tryptophanamide	5000
Threonine deaminase	Threonine	5000
Pyruvate carboxylase	HCO_3^-	1000
	Pyruvate	400
	ATP	60
Cytochrome oxidase	O_2	30

Transformations of the Michaelis-Menten equation—The Michaelis-Menten constant can be algebraically transformed into other forms that are more useful to interpret experimental data. The *Lineweaver-Burk plot* is obtained by relating reciprocals of rates of reaction and substrate concentration, as shown in the following equation:

$$1/V = K_M / V_{max} \times [S] + 1/V_{max} \qquad (22)$$

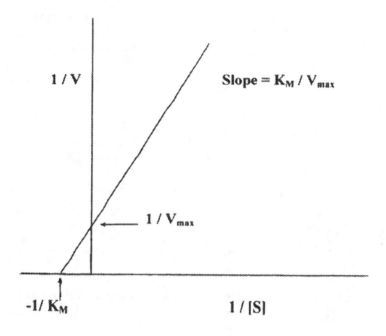

Figure III-5. The Lineweaver-Burk plot of hyperbolical reactions

Another useful transformation of the Michaelis-Menten equation is obtained by arranging the terms in equation 20 to give

$$V = - K_M \times V/[S] + V_{max} \tag{23}$$

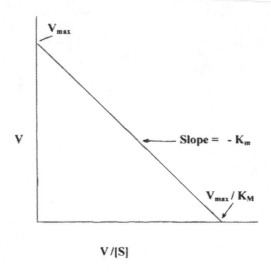

Figure III-6. An Eadie-Hofstee plot of enzyme catalyzed reactions.

A plot of V versus V / [S], called *Eadie-Hofstee plot* not only yields V_{max} and K_M in a very simple way but also magnifies departures from linearity which might not be apparent in the double-reciprocal plot.

The K_M is *equal to the dissociation constant of the ES complex* only when the rate constant k_2 is higher than k_3 (see equation 1). Under these conditions the K_M is a measure of the strength of the ES complex. A *high K_M indicates* low affinity and *weak binding between enzyme and substrate.* Conversely a *low K_M indicates high affinity and strong binding.* It is emphasized that K_M indicates *affinity* of the ES complex only at *low levels of substrate and when k_2 is higher than k_3.*

III. 4. Turnover number and Hill coefficient of enzyme catalyzed reactions

The *turnover number* of an enzyme is defined as the number of molecules of substrate converted into product by a molecule of enzyme per unit time when the enzyme is fully saturated with substrate. The turnover number is best represented by the rate constant

k_3 (see equation # 1). The maximal rate of a reaction, V_{max}, is equal to the turnover number only when the total number of active sites of the enzyme $[E_T]$ is known.

$$\text{Turnover number} = V_{max} = k_3 \times [E_T]$$

The turnover number of most enzymes falls in the range from 0.5 to 10^6 per second.

Table III-2 Maximal turnover numbers of some enzymes

Enzyme	Turnover number (per second)
Carbonic anhydrase	6×10^5
3-Ketosteroid isomerase	2.8×10^5
Acetylcholinesterase	2.5×10^4
Cytochrome oxidase	5×10^3 *
Penicillinase	2×10^3
Lactate dehydrogenase	1,000
ATP hydrolysis	635*
DNA polymerase I	15
Tryptophan synthase	2
Lysozyme	0.5

[* Data extracted from B. Reynafarje and J. Ferreira *J. Bioenerg. Biomembr.* (2002):259-267, and B. Reynafarje and P. Pedersen *J. Biol. Chem.* (1996):32546-32550]

Importantly, when the substrate concentration is much grater than K_M, the rate of catalysis is equal to k_3, the turnover number. However, since under physiological conditions most enzymes are not normally saturated with substrates, the $[S] / K_M$ ratio is typically between 0.01 and 1.0. When $[S] \ll K_M$ the enzymatic rate is much less than k_3 because most of the active sites are unoccupied. Under these conditions the concentration of free enzyme, [E], is nearly equal to the total concentration of enzyme $[E_T]$, and so

$$V = (k_3 / K_M) \times [S] [E_T]$$

Thus, when $[S] \ll K_M$ he enzymatic velocity depends on the value of k_3 / K_M and on [S].

When the rate of formation of product k_3 is much faster than the rate of dissociation of the ES complex (k_2) the vale of k_3 / K_M approaches k_1 (see equation 1). Thus the ultimate limit on the value of k_3 / K_M is set by k_1, the rate of formation of the ES complex.

However, since the rate of formation of the ES complex, k_1, cannot be faster than the diffusion controlled encounter of an enzyme and its substrate, diffusion limits the value of k_1 so that it cannot be higher than between 10^{-8} and 10^{-9} M^{-1} s^{-1}. Hence the upper limit on k_3 / K_M is between 10^{-8} and 10^9 M^{-1} s^{-1}.

Under normal physiological conditions, when the enzyme is saturated with its substrate, the rate of enzymatic activity is known as k_{cat}, which depends on several rate constants rather than on k_3 alone. The pertinent parameter for these enzymes is the k_{ca} / K_M ratio. *Kinetic perfection* is attained when the rate of reaction is only *limited* by the rate at which the substrate encounters the catalytic site(s) of the enzyme. Any further increment in catalytic rate can only come by increasing the rate of diffusion of the substrate. To overcome any limitation in the rates of reaction enzymes are associated in organized assemblies so that the product of one enzyme is very rapidly found by the next enzyme. The organization of enzymes in the inner membrane of the mitochondria is a clear example of the way the cell has to overcome the limitations in the rates of diffusion of electrons and protons during the respiratory process of O_2 reduction to water. Although the rate of diffusion of O_2 from cytosol to matrix limits the rates of O_2 consumption, the confining of electrons, protons and O_2 at the level of the respiratory chain guaranty the maximal rates of reaction. The K_M and V_{max} values of a reaction provide important information concerning the kinetic properties of *hyperbolical* reactions. The value of K_M varies widely depending on all, type of enzyme and substrate, pH, temperature and ionic strength of the medium.

Kinetic properties of allosterically regulated reactions—With few exceptions, like those observed during the catalytic activity of RNA molecules, all known enzymes are proteins. Because enzymes have the capacity to specifically bind a very wide range of molecules, they can determine the pattern of chemical and energy transformations. Thus, by using intermolecular forces, enzymes are able to put substrates in optimal orientations in order to effectively break chemical bonds. The most remarkable characteristics of enzymes are their *catalytic power*, *specificity* and the inherent ability to *regulate* their activity by transferring conformational changes between spatially distinct catalytic sites. The modification in the activity of an enzyme by the binding of a molecule at a site other than the enzymatically active site is known as *allosteric regulation*. In allosteric controlled reactions, catalytic sites come together to form a much more intricate and sentient molecule, so that the binding of a substrate molecule enhances the binding of additional molecules in a *cooperative* type of process. An allosteric enzyme may be *homo-tropic*, when the molecule regulating their activity is the own substrate, *or hetero-tropic*, when the regulating molecule is different than the substrate. Allosteric enzymes do not usually show classic Michaelis-Menten kinetics because the relationship between substrate concentration, velocity (V) and maximal velocity (V_{max}) are greatly altered by the allosteric modulator. In general, allosteric homo-tropic enzymes show *sigmoidal* curves when the rates of reaction are plotted versus the initial concentration of substrate.

During the steepest portion of a sigmoidal curve the rates of reaction are frequently much higher than what is afforded by a simple, non-regulatory enzyme obeying hyperbolical Michaelis-Menten kinetics. Sigmoidal relationships are examples of *positive cooperativity* between multiple sites since the binding of a substrate to the first site enhances the binding of this substrate to the next catalytic site. It should be made clear, however, that not all allosteric enzymes exhibit sigmoid curves when V is plotted versus [S]; moreover, not all enzymes showing such sigmoid curves are necessarily allosteric enzyme. Some allosteric enzymes respond to the binding of a modulator by changing the K_M without changing the V_{max}. In these cases a positive modulator *decreases* the apparent K_M and a negative modulator *increases* the apparent K_M.

Since under these conditions the relationship between V and [S] is not a rectangular hyperbola the term $S_{0.5}$ or EC_{50} is used in sigmoidal reactions instead of "apparent K_M". Allosteric enzymes do not obey Michaelis-Menten kinetics. The initial rates of reaction in sigmoidal reactions are very slow but *exponentially* increase as the substrate concentration increases, to the extent that intermediate rates can be much higher than intermediate rates in hyperbolical reactions.

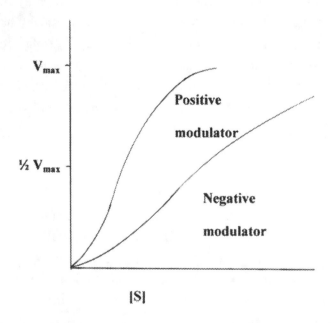

Figure III-7. Changes in the rates of reaction of allosterically regulated enzymes

During the sigmoidal process of ATP synthesis, for example, the very initial rates are almost imperceptible but intermediate rates can be orders of magnitude higher than the hyperbolical rates of ATP hydrolysis.

The Hill coefficient in cooperative type of reactions—The binding of a substrate to an enzyme and the formation of the enzyme-substrate complex, ES, can be described by a simple equilibrium.

$$[ES] = [E] + [S] \tag{1}$$

in which [ES] is the concentration of the enzyme-substrate complex, [E] is the concentration of free enzyme, and [S] is the concentration of *uncombined* substrate.

The degree of saturation, Y, or fractional occupancy of the active sites of an enzyme by its substrate is entirely different in hyperbolical than in sigmoidal type of reactions. In the latter the rates of reaction increase exponentially depending on substrate concentration, and the entire reaction can be most precisely expressed by the Hill equation.

$$Y = (S)^n / (S)^n + (C_{50})^n \tag{2}$$

where C_{50} is the substrate concentration at which 50% of the catalytic sites are filled. This equation states that the ratio of [ES] to [S] is equal to the *nth* power of the ratio of [S] to C_{50}.

Since in hyperbolical reactions the *nth* power is 1.0, the Hill equation can be simply represented by the following equation:

$$Y = (S) / (S) + (C_{50}) \tag{3}$$

In this equation Y = 1.0 when [S] is significantly higher than [C_{50}].

Furthermore, because the fractional occupancy, Y, can range from 0, when all sites are empty, to 1 when all sites are filled we can arrange equation 2 to give

$$Y / 1 - Y = (S / C_{50})^n \qquad (4)$$

Taking logarithms of both sides of equation 4 gives

$$\log Y / 1 - Y = n \log [S] - n \log C_{50} \qquad (5)$$

A plot of $\log Y / 1 - Y$ versus $\log [S]$ always gives a strait line with a slope of 1.0 in hyperbolical reactions and close to 3.0 in sigmoidal reactions. During the activity of the ATP synthase, for example, the *Hill coefficient, n,* is 1.0 for the *hyperbolical process of ATP hydrolysis* and close to 2.9 for the *sigmoidal process of ATP synthesis* (Fig. III-8). The Hill coefficients for the synthesis and hydrolysis of ATP, and for the binding of O_2 to myoglobin and hemoglobin, are respectively shown in figures III-8 and III-9.

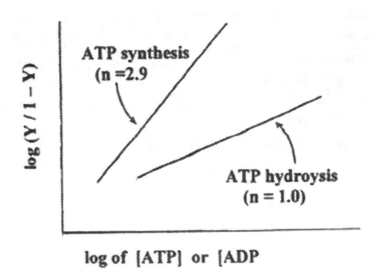

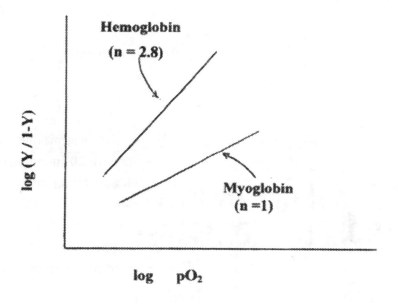

It should be emphasized that, in the oxidative phosphorylation process of ATP synthesis, the Hill coefficient is a constant regardless of any change in redox potential (ΔE_h) and initial concentration of O_2 and ADP. The substrate concentration required for half-maximal rates of the *sigmoidal process of ATP synthesis* (EC_{50}), however, exquisitely depends on ΔE_h and the initial concentration of O_2 and ADP [see Fig. 6 in Int. J. Med. Sci. (2008), 5(3):149]. 43

TRANSPORT OF OXYGEN FROM AIR TO TISSUES

IV. 1. Introduction

A fundamental advance in bioenergetics was attained when it was discovered that the energy released during the respiratory process of electron transport from reduced substrates to O_2 was utilized in the process of ATP synthesis. Although the flow of electrons that take place along the inner mitochondrial membrane is apparently simple, the utilization of the free energy thus generated is extremely complex. Most of the electrons involved in the overall process of oxidative phosphorylation come from NADH and $FADH_2$, which are able to reduce O_2 to water through a series of reactions catalyzed by protein-complexes located inside the cell. In humans, the respiratory process of O_2 consumption is controlled by neural and chemical mechanisms. The spontaneously controlled rhythmic discharges of motor neurons that innervate the respiratory muscles are totally dependent on nerve impulses from the brain to the extent that breathing stops if the spinal cord is transected above the origin of the phrenic nerves. Te neural dependence of the respiratory process is regulated by two separate mechanisms. The *voluntary system*, located in the cerebral cortex, sends impulses to respiratory neurons *via* corticospinal tracts. The *automatic system* is located in the white matter of the spinal cord between the lateral and ventral corticospinal tracts. The chemical regulation of the respiratory process is controlled by alterations in the arterial concentrations of O_2 (pO_2), CO_2 (pCO_2), and protons (pH). The concentration of O_2 and CO_2 is controlled by the gradient of concentrations that exist between lung and tissues. The level of O_2 in the blood *decreases* from a maximum of near 230 μM O_2 (150 torr) at the level of the lungs to a range of values that at tissues level change from a minimum of near zero to a maximum of about 67 μM (45 torr). In the case of CO_2 the partial pressure *decreases* from about 55 mm Hg at the level of the tissues to a minimum of near zero in the inhaled air.

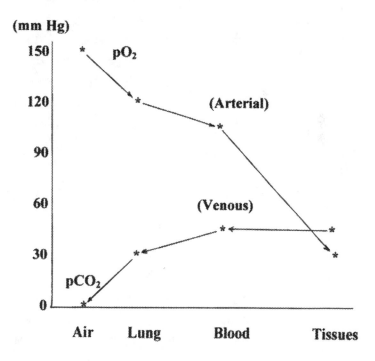

Figure IV-1. Partial pressure of O_2 and CO_2 in torr at the levels of air, lungs, blood and tissues.[After W.F. Ganong. Review of Medical Physiology (1993) p.605]

IV. 2. Transport of oxygen by the cardiovascular system

The O_2 transport system from air to tissues consists of the lungs and the cardiovascular system. The delivery of O_2 to tissues depends on the amount of O_2 entering the lungs, the adequacy of pulmonary gas exchange, the blood flow to the tissues, and the capacity of the blood to carry O_2. The amount of O_2 in the blood is determined by the amount of dissolved O_2, the amount of hemoglobin in the blood, and the affinity of this protein for O_2. *Hemoglobin*, the oxygen-carrying pigment in the red blood cells of vertebrates, is a protein made up of 4 subunits with a molecular weight of 64,450. Each subunit contains an iron atom per heme moiety able to reversible bind one O_2 molecule. The polypeptides are referred to collectively as the *globin* portion of the hemoglobin. The *functional unity of hemoglobin is a tetramer consisting of 2α and 2 β kinds of polypeptide chains.*

Because the redox-state of iron during the transport of O_2 remains in the ferrous state, the *binding of O_2 to hemoglobin is an oxygenation, not an oxidation.* Therefore the binding of one molecule of O_2 per atom of iron result in the sequential binding and transport of 4 molecules of O_2 in a form that goes from Hb_4O_2 to Hb_4O_8.

$$Hb_4 + O_2 === Hb_4O_2$$
$$Hb_4O_2 + O_2 === Hb_4O_4$$
$$Hb_4O_4 + O_2 === Hb_4O_6$$
$$Hb_4O_6 + O_2 === Hb_4O_8$$

The oxygenation of Hb_4 and the complete deoxygenation (reduction) of Hb_4O_8 takes place in less than 0.01 seconds. By shifting the relationship of its 4 component polypeptide chains, a molecule of hemoglobin determines its affinity for O_2. The quaternary structure of hemoglobin facilitates either the uptake or deliver of O_2. The movement of the chains is associated with a change in the position of the heme moieties, which assume a *relaxed or R state,* that favors O_2 binding, or a *tense or T state* that decreases O_2 binding. The transition from one state to another involves the formation and the braking of bridges between the polypeptide chains. It has been calculated that these shifts occur about 10^8 times in the life of a red blood cell. The correlation between the partial pressure of O_2 (pO_2) and the saturation of the four hemes of hemoglobin with O_2 is generally known as the *oxygen dissociation curve of hemoglobin*, which is sigmoidal in shape

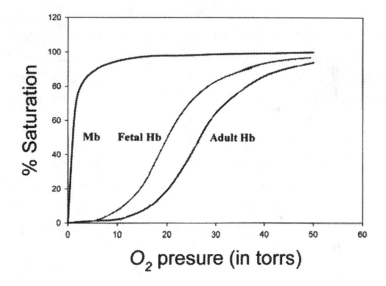

Figure IV-2. Oxygen dissociation curves of myoglobin and hemoglobin both Fetal and Adult.

The binding of O_2 to the first heme increases the affinity of the second heme for O_2, and the binding of O_2 to the second heme increases the affinity of the third, in such a way that the affinity of the fourth for O_2 is many times higher than the affinity of the first for O_2. On the contrary, the unloading of O_2 from one heme facilitates the unloading from the other sites. This type of cooperativity between hemes makes hemoglobin the most efficient oxygen transporter.

Although the α and β subunits of Hb have the same structural design as myoglobin (Mb), the tetramer of hemoglobin is a much more intricate and sentient molecule than Mb. Because the interaction between separate, nonadjacent sites of hemoglobin are regulated by organic phosphates such as 2,3-phosphoglycerate (BPG), the oxygen-binding affinity of hemoglobin is much lower than the affinity of myoglobin for O_2. Furthermore, hemoglobin transports not only O_2 but H^+ and CO_2 as well. Any increment in the concentration of H^+ and CO_2 promotes the release of O_2 from hemoglobin and *vice versa*, any increment in O_2 concentration promotes the release of H^+ and CO_2.

Due to a slight admixture with venous blood that bypasses the lungs (physiologic shunt) the saturation of hemoglobin with O_2 in systemic arterial blood is close to 97%. The arterial blood therefore contains a total of 19.8 ml of O_2 per deciliter, with 0.29 ml in solution and 19.5 ml bound to hemoglobin. In venous blood at rest, the hemoglobin is 75% saturated with O_2 and the total O_2 content is 15.2 ml of O_2 per 100 ml of blood, with 15.08 ml bound to hemoglobin and 0.12 ml in solution. Thus, at rest the tissues remove close to 4.6 ml of O_2 per deciliter of blood (19.8 ml of O_2 arriving in arterial capillaries and 15.2 ml of O_2 returning in venous capillaries per deciliter of blood passing all tissues.

This means that close to 260 ml of O_2 are delivered from a total of 5,600 ml of blood containing close to 15 gm. of hemoglobin per deciliter in men and somewhat lower in women.

Mechanistically significant is the fact that the β chains of hemoglobin move closer together during the binding of O_2 and further apart during its release. The affinity of hemoglobin for O_2 changes also depending on the temperature and environmental concentration of O_2. At sea level and a barometric pressure of 760 mm Hg, when the pO_2 in the air is 150 torr and the concentration of O_2 in water is ~230 μM O_2, half maximal saturation of hemoglobin with O_2 is attained at a pO_2 of 26 torr or 40 μM (see figure IV-2). Under the hypoxic conditions of high altitudes, the affinity of hemoglobin for O_2 decreases in order to facilitate the release of O_2 to the tissues. Furthermore, since O_2 diffuses from to the cytosolic to the matrix side of mitochondria driven by a gradient of O_2 concentrations, it is evident that the level of O_2 in contact with the cytochrome oxidase is no higher than 76 µM, which is the maximal level inside the cells.

Table IV -1. Translocation of O_2 in solution from air to tissue

O_2 available	% Saturation	pO_2 (torr)	ml O_2 per 100 ml of blood	$[O_2]$ in solution
Air		150		230 µM
Lung				
Air		108		166 µM
Arterial (bound to Hb)	97.0		19.50	
Arterial serum		95	0.29	146 µM
Total O_2 content			19.8	
Venous (bound to Hb)	75.0		15.10	
Venous serum		40	0.12	53.6 µM
Total O_2 content			5.22	
O_2 delivered to tissue			0.17	75.9 µM

IV. 3. Physiological transport of O_2 form blood to mitochondria

Hemoglobin (Hb) and myoglobin (Mb) are essential proteins respectively involved in the transport and storage of oxygen. Hemoglobin contained in red blood cells plays a vital role in the transport not only of O_2 but H^+ and CO_2 as well. The binding of O_2 to hemoglobin is exquisitely regulated by the concentration of organic phosphates (2, 3-diphosphoglycerate, 2, 3-bisphosphoglycerate, DPG or BPG), H^+ and CO_2. These regulators greatly affect the oxygen-binding properties of hemoglobin by binding to sites far from the actual binding site for O_2. BPG, a highly anionic organic phosphate, is present in human red cells at about the same molar concentration as hemoglobin.

DPG and H^+ compete with O_2 to bind the *deoxygenated* form of hemoglobin by decreasing the affinity for O_2 of the quaternary structure of its 4 polypeptide chains. At the level of the lungs, when the levels of CO_2 and H^+ *decrease*, the oxygen dissociation curve of hemoglobin shifts to the left *increasing* the affinity of hemoglobin for O_2. At tissues level, when the concentrations of CO_2 and H^+ *increases*, the oxygen dissociation curve of hemoglobin shifts to the right *decreasing* its affinity for O_2 and facilitating its release. The effect of CO_2, H^+ and DPG on the affinity of hemoglobin for O_2 is known as *Bohr Effect*.

Although the structural design of myoglobin is similar to the structure of the *isolated* α and β chains of hemoglobin, myoglobin lacks the allosteric property of hemoglobin to change its affinity for O_2 depending on the levels of pH, CO_2 and DPG. The *affinity of myoglobin* for O_2 is not affected by the concentrations of CO_2 and DGP or the pH. Distinctly, DPG is the most important modulator of the *affinity of hemoglobin* for O_2. In the absence of DPG hemoglobin, like myoglobin, attains 50 % saturation with O_2 at a pO_2 of only 1 torr or 1.5 μM O_2. However, in the presence of DPG hemoglobin attains 50% saturation at a pO_2 of 26 torr or 40 μM O_2. It is physiological significant that the binding and release of O_2 to and from hemoglobin is *sigmoidal* in nature. The binding and release of O_2 from one heme facilitates the binding and unloading from the other sites. Distinctly, the O_2 binding of myoglobin is *hyperbolical* and the heme remains saturated with O_2 until the concentration of O_2 inside the cell falls far bellow 10 μM.

The oxygen dissociation curve of *fetal* hemoglobin, F, *shits to the left in order to increase the affinity of hemoglobin for O_2 and to facilitate the binding of O_2 at the fetal side of the placenta.* Fetal hemoglobin and adult hemoglobin are structurally different. While hemoglobin A has 2α and 2β polypeptide chains, hemoglobin F has

2α and 2γ polypeptide chains. Consequently, 50% saturation of fetal hemoglobin is attained at a pO_2 of about 20 torr ($\sim$30.7 μM O_2) rather than 26 torr.

During the process of adaptation to the hypoxic environments of high altitude *the oxygen dissociation curve of hemoglobin shifts to the right thus decreasing the affinity of hemoglobin for O_2 and facilitating its release at tissues level.* Indeed at an altitude of 4,500 m, when the barometric pressure is equal to 450 mm Hg and the pO_2 is only 80 torr, the oxygen dissociation curve of hemoglobin is $\sim$30 torr (46 μM O_2) rather than 26 torr at se level. However, since the binding of O_2 by Hb depends on the environmental level of O_2 (close to 1.34 ml of O_2 per gm of Hb at sea level) the extent of Hb in the blood of natives to high altitude is significantly increased to compensate the lower environmental concentrations of O_2

Although the three-dimensional structure of the single chain in myoglobin is identical to the three-dimensional structures of the four chains in hemoglobin (particularly to the β chain), the oxygen dissociation curves of myoglobin and hemoglobin are entirely different. Regardless of O_2 concentration, the oxygen dissociation curve *of myoglobin is hyperbolical whereas that of hemoglobin is sigmoidal* (see figure IV-2). Thus, while the Hill coefficient of myoglobin is only 1.0 the Hill coefficient of hemoglobin is close to 3.0.

Considering that the fractional occupancy, *Y*, of the active sites in both hemoglobin and myoglobin range from 0, when all sites are empty, to 1.0 when all sites are filed, the binding of oxygen to myoglobin (Mb) can be described by the following hypothetical equation.

$$MbO_2 = Mb + O_2 \tag{1}$$

The equilibrium constant K_{eq} for the dissociation of oxymyoglobin (MbO_2) would be

$$K_{eq} = [Mb]\,[O_2]\,/\,MbO_2 \tag{2}$$

where the concentrations of deoxymyoglobin [Mb], and [O_2] are given in moles per liter. The fractional occupancy of a binding site of myoglobin would be:

$$Y = MbO_2 / [MbO_2] + [Mb] \qquad (3)$$

Substitution of equation 2 into equation 3 yields

$$Y = [O_2] / [O_2] + K_{eq} \qquad (4)$$

Expressing the concentration of O_2 in terms of the partial pressure of O_2 in torr units and using P_{50} instead of K_{eq}, equation 4 becomes:

$$Y = pO_2 / pO_2 + P_{50} \qquad (5)$$

A plot of the fractional occupancy (Y) versus the ratio of $pO_2/pO_2 + P_{50}$, closely matches the experimentally observed curve for myoglobin with an O_2 dissociation curve, P_{50}, that is close to 1.5 torr or 2.3 μM O_2.

On the other hand, the binding of oxygen to hemoglobin can be derived from the following equilibrium.

$$Hb(O_2)_n = Hb + nO_2 \qquad (6)$$

The value of Y for equation 6 can be derived to yield

$$Y = (pO_2)^n / (pO_2)^n + (P_{50})^n \qquad (7)$$

which can be rearranged to give

$$Y/1 - Y = (pO_2 / P_{50})^n \qquad (8)$$

This equation states that the ratio of oxyhemoglobin (Y) to deoxyhemoglobin (1-Y) is equal to the nth power of the ratio of pO_2 to P_{50}. Taking logarithms on both sides of this equation

$$\log Y/1\text{-}Y = n \log pO_2 - n \log P_{50} \qquad (9)$$

Plots of log $[Y/(1 - Y)]$ versus log pO_2 result in straight lines. The *Hill coefficient, n*, depends directly on the degree of cooperativity between binding sites (see Figs. III-8 & 9).

THE RESPIRATORY ROCESS OF O2 CONSUMPTION

V. 1. Introduction

Most of the free energy that supports the life of aerobic organisms is released during the mitochondrial process of oxidative-phosphorylation when oxygen is reduced to water with electrons and protons coming from reduced respiratory substrates. The generation of metabolic energy in humans is the expression of 84 key genes, including those that encode the mitochondrial complexes of electron transport and oxidative phosphorylation. The electrons that finally reduce oxygen come from NADH and $FADH_2$, which are energy-reach molecules formed during the oxidation of glucose, fatty acids and amino acids. Each, NADH and $FADH_2$ contain a pair of high-transfer potential electrons that by reducing O_2 at the level of cytochrome oxidase release the free energy that is utilized by the ATP-synthase to synthesize ATP, the currency of metabolic energy in aerobic cells.

V. 2. Components of the mitochondrial membranes

Mitochondria (also called *chondriosomes*) are spherical or elongated organelles located in the cytoplasm of nearly all eukaryotic cells. The genetic material contained in mitochondria, together with the enzymes in charge to convert food stuff into usable forms of energy such as ATP, are essential for the energy metabolism of the cell. The number of mitochondria depends on the cell's function. Cells with particularly heavy energy demands, such as muscle cells, have more mitochondria than other cells. The mitochondrial volume makes close to 20% of liver cells and up to 50% of heart cells. Mitochondria have two membrane systems: an *outer membrane* and an extensive, highly folded *inner membrane* that forms ridges called *cristae*. The outer and the inner membranes separate two distinct spaces: the *intermembrane space* and the *matrix space*. The latter contains most of the enzymes involved in the oxidation of fatty acids, the components of the citric acid cycle or Krebs cycle and the mitochondrial deoxyribonucleic acid (mtDNA) directly involved in protein synthesis. Among animals, mitochondria tend to follow a pattern of maternal inheritance. The mitochondrial matrix also contains ribosomes, which are minute round particles composed of RNA and protein located near the portion of the inner membrane that is most closely related to the outer membrane. The *cristae*, the number of which depends on the type of cell, appear to be devices necessary to *increase the surface area of the inner membrane without affecting the volume of the whole mitochondria. The structure of the cristae is considered to be directly involved in the physiological process of ATP synthesis.* In contrast with the outer membrane, the inner membrane is intrinsically impermeable to nearly all ions and polar molecules. A large family of shuttles is involved in the transfer of metabolites such as ATP and citrate across the inner mitochondrial membrane. More than six decades ago, Eugene Kennedy and Albert Lehninger discovered that mitochondria contain the respiratory assembly and the enzymes of the citric acid cycle and fatty acid oxidation responsible for the endergonic process of ATP synthesis. The localization of enzymes in rat liver mitochondria is illustrated below:

Table V-1. Components of the mitochondrial membranes

Outer membrane:
Monoamino oxidase
Kynunerine 3-monooxigenase
Antimycine-insensitive NADH dehydrogenase
Acyl-CoA synthase
Phospholipase A_2
Nucleoside diphosphate kinase

Intermembrane space
Adenylate kinase

Inner membrane
NADH dehydrogenase (antimycin-sensitive)
Iron-sulfur proteins
Succinate dehydrogenase
D-β-Hydroxybutyrate dehydrogenase
Cytochromes *b, c, c_1 and aa_3*
ATP synthase
Carnitine acyltransferase

Matrix (Enzymes of the citric acid cycle (Krebs cycle))
Oxidative decarboxilation of pyruvate
Citrate synthase
Aconitase
Isocitrate dehydrogenase
α-keto-glutarate
Succinyl CoA synthase
Succinate dehydrogenase
Fumarase
Malate dehydrogenase
Glutamate dehydrogenase
Aspartate transsaminase
Fatty acyl-CoA oxidation enzymes

V. 3. Complexes of the respiratory chain

The driving force for the oxidative phosphorylation process of ATP synthesis is provided by the free energy released at the level of the components of the respiratory chain during the transport of electrons from NADH and $FADH_2$ to oxygen. The active transport system of the respiratory chain is formed by iron and copper ions contained in transmembrane complexes of flavins, iron-sulfur clusters (Fe-S) and hemes. The protein complexes are *NADH-Q reductase or NADH dehydrogenase (complex I), succinate-Q reductase (complex II), cytochrome reductase (complex III), and cytochrome oxidase (complex IV)*. A fifth protein complex of the inner mitochondrial membrane is the *ATP-synthase (complex V)*, which is in charge to catalyze the synthesis of ATP.

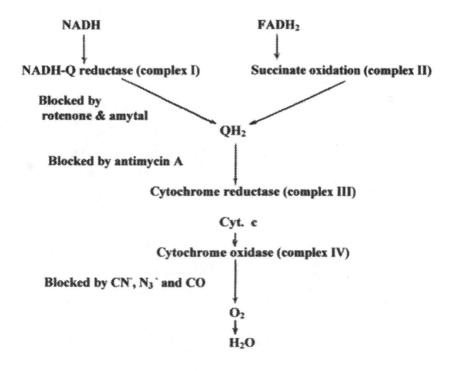

Figure V-1, Complexes of the respiratory chain.

The use of specific inhibitors revealed the sequence in the flow of electrons from fully reduced substrates to O_2. The most important of these inhibitors are *amytal, rotenone, antimycin, CN⁻, N_3^- and CO*. Amytal and rotenone block electrons transfer at the level of the NADH-Q reductase. While azide and cyanide react with the ferric form of *heme a_3*, carbon monoxide inhibits its ferrous form.

The following Table shows the flow of electrons through the chain of four large protein complexes and its prosthetic groups.

Table V-2. Prosthetic groups of the mitochondrial enzyme complexes

Enzyme complex	Prosthetic group
NADH-Q reductase (complex I)	FMN
	Fe-S (4Fe-4S & 2Fe-2S)
Succinate-reductase (complex II)	FAD
	Fe-S
Cytochrome reductase (complex III)	Heme b-562
	Heme b-566
	Heme c_1
	Fe-S
Cytochrome oxidase (complex IV)	Heme a (Fe^{+2} & Fe^{+3})
	Heme a_3 (Fe^{+2} & Fe^{+3})
	Cu_A and Cu_B (Cu^{+1} & Cu^{+2})

Electrons of *NADH-Q reductase* (also called *NADH dehydrogenase*), a large enzyme of 880 kd, consisting of at least 34 polypeptide chains. The initial step is the binding of NADH and the transfer of its two high-potential electrons to the *flavin mononucleotide* (*FMN*) prosthetic group of this complex to give the reduced form, $FMNH_2$.

$$NADH + H^+ + FMN = FMNH_2. + NAD^+$$

74

V. 4. 1.14 volts drives the transfer of electrons from NADH to O_2 via QH_2

Electrons from complex I and complex II are transferred to complex III by the reduced form of *ubiquinol (Q)*, a hydrophobic quinone that diffuses rapidly within the inner mitochondrial membrane. Cytochrome *c*, a small protein, shuttles electrons from complex III to complex IV, which is the final component of the respiratory chain. All complexes, except complex II are able to pump protons from the matrix to the cytosolic side of mitochondria. Complex I, which is a large L-shaped enzyme of 880 kd, consists of at least 34 polypeptide chains that cross the inner-mitochondrial membrane and is encoded by two genomes: nuclear and mitochondrial. Only a portion of complex I projects into the matrix of mitochondria where electrons contained in NADH are first transferred to FMN. Electrons are transferred inside the complex to three [4Fe-4S] centers and then to tightly bound Q. The pair of electrons in QH_2 are transferred to a [2Fe-2Fe] center, and finally, to a mobile Q in the hydrophobic core of the membrane.

The free energy released during the flow of electrons from respiratory substrates (NADH or $FADH_2$) to oxygen is not at all affected by the level of ADP or the phosphorylative process of ATP synthesis. The extent and rates of electron flow are exquisite functions of the level of O_2 and the degree of reduction of cytochrome aa_3.

The intrinsic and indispensable driving force for the oxidative phosphorylation process of ATP synthesis is the electron transfer potential between NADH or $FADH_2$ and O_2. Thus, since the actual standard free energy change $(\Delta E'_o)$ for the following half-reactions is equal to:

$$\tfrac{1}{2}\,O_2 + 2H^+ + 2e^- = H_2O \qquad\qquad \Delta E'_o = +0.82 \text{ V}$$
$$NAD^+ + 2H^+ + 2e^- = NADH + H^+ \qquad\qquad \Delta E'_o = -0.32 \text{ V}$$
$$NADP^+ + 2H^+ + 2e^- = NADPH + H^+ \qquad\qquad \Delta E'_o = -0.32 \text{ V}$$

The $\Delta E_o^{'}$ for the flow of electrons from NADH or NADPH to O_2 is:

$$\tfrac{1}{2}O_2 + NADH + H^+ = H_2O + NAD^+ \qquad \Delta E_o^{'} = +0.816 - (-0.32) = +1.14 \text{ V}.$$

In fact, the oxidation of NADH or NADPH generates a $\Delta E_o^{'}$ of +1.14 V which is equal to the mitochondrial free energy change ($\Delta G^{0'}$) of -52.6 kcal/mol ($\Delta G^{0'} = -n/F\Delta E_o^{'} = -2 \times 23.06 \times 1.14 = -52.6$ kcal/mol), enough to support the synthesis of more than 3 molecules of ATP.

The first phase in the flow of electrons is the binding of NADH to the NADH-Q reductase of complex I and the consequent transfer of its two high-potential electrons to the flavin mononucleotide (FMN), resulting in its reduction and the formation of $FMNH_2$

$$NADH + H^+ + FMN = NAD^+ + FMNH_2$$

The second phase in the flow of electrons is the transfer to a series of *iron-sulfur clusters* (Fe-S), the second type of prosthetic group in NADH-Q reductase or complex I. Iron-sulfur clusters in non-heme iron-sulfur proteins play a critical role in a wide range of reduction reactions in biological systems. In its simplest form a Fe-S cluster only contains a single iron atom. A second type of iron-sulfur cluster is the one containing 2 iron atoms and two inorganic sulfides (2Fe-sS) in addition to four cysteine residues. A third type, designated as (4Fe-4S), contains four iron atoms, four inorganic sulfides, and four cysteine residues. Complex I contain both [2Fe-2S] and [4Fe-4S] clusters. Iron atoms in these clusters cycle between reduced (Fe^{2+}) and oxidized (Fe^{3+}) states.

Electrons in the iron-sulfur clusters of NADH-Q reductase or complex I are then shuttled to *coenzyme Q*, also called ubiquinone Q because it is ubiquitous in biological systems. The most common form in mammals contains 10 isoprene units (Q_{10}). Ubiquinone is reduced to a free-radical semiquinone anion (Q^-) by the uptake of a single electron. The total reduction of this enzyme-bound intermediate by a second electron yields *ubiquinol (QH₂)*.

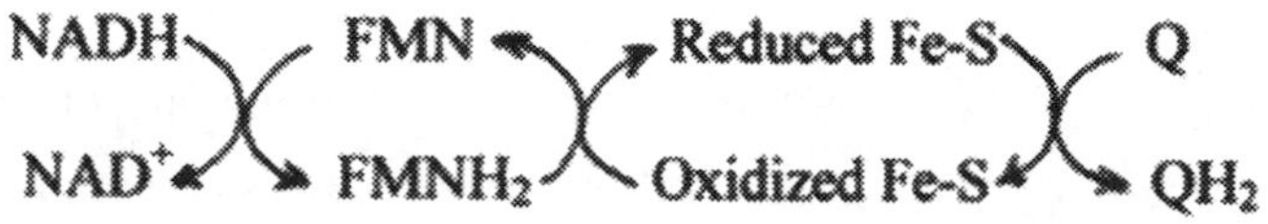

NADH⟍ ⟋ FMN ← ⟍ Reduced Fe-S⟍ ⟋ Q

NAD⁺← ⟍ FMNH₂ ⟋ ⟍ Oxidized Fe-S ← ⟍ QH₂

Figure V-2. The reduction of coenzyme Q by NADH

Electrons from NADH enter complex I at the level of FMN to reduce first three 4Fe-4S clusters on the vertical or hydrophilic core of complex I and then to a tightly bound Q. The electrons in the resulting bound QH_2 are transferred to a [2Fe-2S] center, and finally to reduce a mobile form of Q to ubiquinol (QH_2) in the hydrophobic core of the membrane. *Coenzyme Q is also the entry site for electrons coming from* $FADH_2$ *which is formed at the level of* succinate-Q reductase (Complex II), as well at the level of *fatty acyl CoA*, and α-ketoglutarate dehydrogenases, which are part of the citric acid cycle. These dehydrogenases, in contrast with the NADH-Q reductase, are not proton pumps and the extent of free energy generated during the oxidation of their respective substrates is somehow less than that generated during the oxidation of NADH.

Electrons from ubiquinol (QH_2) are transferred to *Complex III, also called cytochrome reductase, ubiquinol-cytochrome c reductase* or *cytochrome bc₁ complex*. This complex has four key redox centers. Cytochrome *b* with two hemes b_H and b_L, and an iron-sulfur portion with a 2Fe-2S center, and cytochrome c_1 with a single heme. Electrons from QH_2 enter the complex at a site between b_L and 2Fe-2S. They are finally transferred from the c_1 heme to cytochrome *c*, which approaches the complex from the cytosolic side.

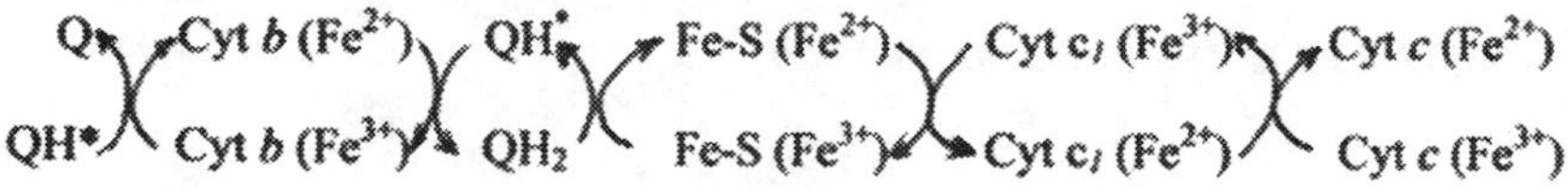

$$Q \underset{QH^\bullet}{\overset{Cyt\ b\ (Fe^{2+})}{\bowtie}} \underset{Cyt\ b\ (Fe^{3+})}{} QH^\bullet_\bullet \underset{QH_2}{\overset{Fe\text{-}S\ (Fe^{2+})}{\bowtie}} \underset{Fe\text{-}S\ (Fe^{3+})}{} \underset{Cyt\ c_l\ (Fe^{2+})}{\overset{Cyt\ c_l\ (Fe^{3+})}{\bowtie}} \underset{Cyt\ c\ (Fe^{3+})}{\overset{Cyt\ c\ (Fe^{2+})}{\bowtie}}$$

Figure V-3. The flow of electrons from coenzyme Q to cytochrome c via the cytochrome reductase or complex III [After Stryer, Biochemistry (1996):536-537].

The function of *cytochrome reductase* or complex III is to catalyze the transfer of electrons from QH_2 to *cytochrome c*, which is a water-soluble protein that contains a heme prosthetic group with the same reduction potential of $+ 0.25$ V in all types of species. The iron atoms of cytochrome c alternate between a reduced ferrous (+2) state and an oxidized ferric (+3) state during electron transport. The flow of a pair of electrons through complex III lead to the effective net transport of 2 protons to the cytosolic side, half the yield obtained with NADH-Q reductase because of a smaller thermodynamic driving force.

V. 5. Cytochrome aa_3 catalyzes the transfer of electrons from cytochrome c to O_2

The final phase in the flow of electrons from NADH to O_2 is catalyzed by Complex IV, *cytochrome c oxidase* or *cytochrome aa_3*. This enzyme catalyzes the translocation of electrons from reduced molecules of cytochrome c (Fe^{2+}) to molecular oxygen

$$4\ Cyt\ c\ (Fe^{2+}) + 4\ H^+ + O_2 = 4\ Cyt\ c\ (Fe^{3+}) + 2\ H_2O$$

This reaction is carried out by a complex of 10 subunits, of which subunits I, II and III are encoded by the mitochondrial genome. Cytochrome oxidase contains two *heme groups and two copper ions*. The *hemes* groups, known as *heme-a* and *heme-a_3*, differ from the hemes in cytochrome c and cytochrome c_1 because they are located in different parts of the enzyme. Likewise, the two copper ions, called Cu_A and Cu_B, are distinct because they are bound differently by the protein. Heme a_3 is next to Cu_B in subunit I, which is closer to the matrix and the oxygen-binding side of cytochrome oxidase. The role of Cu_A is to function as an efficient interface from the hydrophilic substrate ferro-cytochrome c to the more hydrophobic side of the oxidase which is well within the lipid bilayer. The distance between the binding site of cytochrome c and cytochrome c and Cu_A in the cytochrome oxidase would not be much higher than 5 A°.

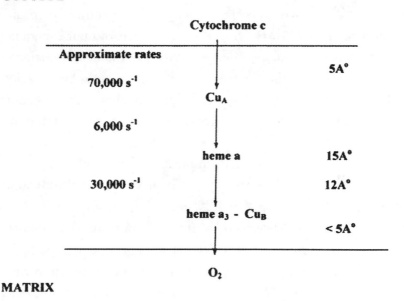

CYTOSOL

Cytochrome c

Approximate rates

70,000 s⁻¹ → Cu_A — 5A°

6,000 s⁻¹

heme a — 15A° / 12A°

30,000 s⁻¹

heme a₃ - Cu_B — < 5A°

O_2

MATRIX

Figure V-4. Distance between Cytochrome c, the components of Cytochrome aa_3 and O_2 [After B.C. Hill. *J. Biol. Chem.* (1991) 266, 2219-2226]

Oxygen, like Fe^{3+}, is an ideal acceptor for electrons flowing through the respiratory chain. The high affinity of O_2 for electrons and protons provides a large thermodynamic driving force, $\Delta G^{o'}$, for the oxidative phosphorylation process of ATP synthesis. This affinity, however, is significantly reduced when the concentration of O_2 is in great excess over the concentration of electrons and protons. Thus, under classic state-3 metabolic conditions, when the concentration of O_2 is close to 230 μM, the rates of O_2 consumption are greatly impaired due to the presence of O_2 radicals such as *superoxide anion*:

$$O_2 + e^- = O_2^-$$

These radicals are potentially destructive compounds. Under normal physiological conditions the concentration of O_2 inside the cell normally changes within a narrow range of concentrations (near zero to a maximum of 70 μM). Only at *in vivo* levels of O_2 the cytochrome aa_3 can become optimally reduced to catalyze the fast reduction of O_2 to water. In reality, the four-electron reduction steps that take place in the redox cycle of cytochrome oxidase begins with the reduction of Fe^{3+}- Cu^{2+} to Fe^{3+}- Cu^+ followed by the reduction of this center to Fe^{2+}- Cu^+. The iron ion of this fully reduced center then binds a molecule of O_2 which abstracts an electron from both ions to form a *peroxy intermediate* with two O^-. The input of a third electron and the uptake of two H^+ lead to the cleavage of the bound peroxide and the formation of a *ferryl intermediate* in which one atom of O_2 is bound to Fe^{4+} in the form of O^{2-} an the other atom is bound to Cu^{2+} in the form of H_2O. The input of the fourth electron and the uptake of two more H^+ result in the safe release of two molecules of H_2O and the regeneration of the oxidized bimetallic center ready to receive more electrons. The transfer of 4 electrons, as shown in figure V-5, leads to the safe formation of two molecules of H_2O through the formation of hazardous *superoxide anion*, which is a potentially destructive compound formed in the presence of abnormally high levels of O_2. It is evident that the uninterrupted flow of electrons and the consequent reduction of O_2 to water *require a constant but limited level of oxygen to avoid the accumulation of impairing oxygen radicals.*

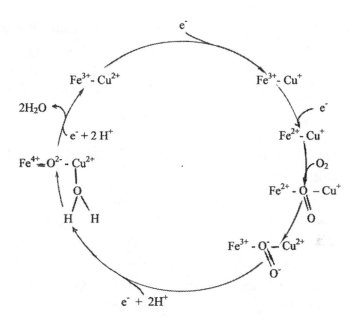

Figure V-5. Flow of electrons from cytochrome *c* to O_2 *via* the cytochrome oxidase [Modified from M. Wikstrom and J.E. Morgan. *J. Biol. Chem.* 267 (1992): 1026].

The release of free energy that is involved in the oxidative phosphorylation process of ATP synthesis requires the *continuous availability of electrons, H^+ and O_2 on the condition that the accumulation of impairing O_2 radicals is extremely low*. This condition is only attained when the respiratory process of O_2 consumption occurs in the presence of *in vivo* levels of O_2, i.e. when under normal physiological conditions the concentration of O_2 is no higher than 70 μM. In reality, the *net synthesis of ATP precedes the net ejection of H^+ and coincides with the net hydrolysis* (not the synthesis) of any previously formed ATP and the *net reduction* (not the oxidation) of cytochrome aa_3 (see figures V-7 and VI-3).

To this day, however, it is still believed that close to 4 H^+ per site of the respiratory chain are transferred from the matrix to the cytosolic side of the respiratory chain during the reduction of an atom of O_2

to water. However, recent experimental evidence demonstrate that, regardless of ADP concentration, net ejection of H^+ only occurs after the extremely fast and hyperbolical phase of O_2 consumption that is directly involved in the phosphorylative process of ATP synthesis (see figures V-7 and VI-3).

V. 6. Metabolic states of mitochondria and the concept of respiratory control

Ever since Chance described the metabolic states of mitochondria it is believed that *maximal rates* of O_2 reduction can only occur under state-3 metabolic conditions in reactions initiated by adding ADP to mostly oxidized mitochondria the presence of ~230 μM O_2 (see Fig.V-6). Under these conditions, however, the rates of both O_2 consumption and ATP synthesis are orders of magnitude lower than under close to *in vivo* concentrations of O_2 that normally vary from nearly zero to a maximum of ~70 μM. In the presence of ~230 μM O_2 the rates of both O_2 consumption and ATP synthesis are greatly reduced by the excess of O_2 and impairing oxygen radicals.

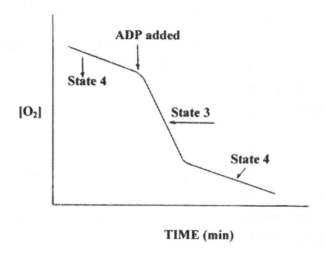

Figure V-6. Rates of O_2 consumption under classic state-3 metabolic condition

The apparently high rates of O_2 uptake observed under classic state-3 metabolic condition are most likely due to the *incomplete* reduction of the mitochondrial membrane induced by the binding of ADP to oxidized mitochondria slowly respiring under state-4 conditions. Entirely different, real rates of O_2 consumption and ATP synthesis only occur when O_2, induced by a gradient of concentrations, diffuses from cytosol to matrix to bind a fully reduced form of cytochrome aa_3 already in the presence of ADP (see Fig. V-7)

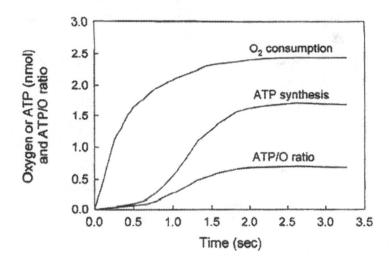

Figure V-7. The oxidative phosphorylation of ATP synthesis *begins with the binding of O_2 to cytochrome aa_3.*

Evidently, the phosphorylative process of ATP synthesis does not *precedes but follows the process of O_2 reduction to water.* In fact, the respiratory process of O_2 consumption in humans is controlled by chemoreceptors and reflexes in breathing, and the *hyperbolical and exergonic process of O_2 consumption controls the sigmoidal and endergonic process of ATP synthesis.*

Under *absolute resting conditions*, when the levels of O_2 and ATP are maximal and the gradient of O_2 concentrations between cytosol and matrix is close to zero, the rates of O_2 uptake and ATP synthesis are *minimal* and just enough to maintain the homeostasis of the cell. Conversely, *after intense physical exercise*, when the levels of both ATP and O_2 are *minimal* and the level of ADP and degree of reduction of cytochrome aa_3 are *maximal*, the rates of ATP synthesis attain *maximal* values the instant in which O_2 is made available (see Fig. V 7).

Table V-3. Metabolic States of Mitochondria and
Redox-state of Related Respiratory Enzymes [Data modified
from B. Chance in *Advances in Enzymology* (1956): XVII, 65-130]

State	$[O_2]$ level	Reduced substrate level	Rate-limiting factor	a	c	b	Flavin	DPNH
						% reduction of		
1	0	low	O_2	100	100	100	150	100
2	>0	high	ADP	0	7	17	21	~90
3	>0	high	O_2 and substrates	<4	6	16	20	53

The metabolic state-1, which is equivalent to the classic state-5, represents the physiological state that occur after an abrupt and intense expenditure of expenditure, when the concentration of O_2 is close to zero and the membrane is fully reduced. The metabolic state-2 of mitochondria, equivalent to the classic state-4, represents the idling period during which the metabolic state of the cell is at rest and the mitochondrial membrane is for the most part oxidized and saturated with O_2. During this state (see second portion in Fig. V-6), the net synthesis of ATP is limited by the lack of ADP and the slow rates of electron flow. Actually, *the most important factor in controlling the respiratory process of O_2 consumption is not the level of ADP but the concentration of O_2 and the degree of reduction and/or protonation of the mitochondrial membrane and cytochrome aa_3.*

Considering that the rates of O_2 uptake under state-3 metabolic conditions can increase up to 10 times when ADP is added to mitochondria respiring under state-4 conditions, it is asserted that the process of ATP synthesis regulates the extent and rates of O_2 consumption. Hence, the term *"respiratory control"* is used to indicate that the oxidative phosphorylation of ATP synthesis control the respiratory processes of electron flow and O_2 consumption. In accordance with this concept it is stated in a reputable textbook that *"electrons do not usually flow through the electron transport chain to O_2 unless ADP is simultaneously phosphorylated to ATP"*. In other words, *electrons do not flow from fuel molecules to O_2 if ADP is not concomitantly phosphorylated to ATP*. Thus, it is believed that maximal rates of electron flow, O_2 uptake and ATP synthesis only occur under state-3 metabolic conditions in reactions initiated by adding ADP to mostly oxidized mitochondria respiring in the presence of abnormally high levels of O_2 (>200 µM). Under these conditions, however, there is no strict correlation between the respiratory process of O_2 consumption and the phosphorylative of ATP synthesis. Strict kinetic and thermodynamic correlation between these two processes only occurs during the first phase of oxidative phosphorylation that, resembling *in vitro* O_2-pulse experiments, begins with the net oxidation of previously reduced cytochrome aa_3. In reality, *the processes of electron flow and O_2 reduction to water control the level of ADP and the process of ATP synthesis, not vice versa*. Under normal physiological conditions, the free energy of electron flow is released during the first milliseconds of the *hyperbolical process of O_2 consumption. The sigmoidal process of ATP synthesis is the consequence* of the respiratory process of O_2 reduction (see Fig. V-7).

Regardless of the magnitude of the ΔE_h, the concentration of ADP (endogenous or externally added), the form and concentration of mitochondria (homogenates of whole tissues, intact mitochondria or inverted inner-mitochondrial vesicles), the oxidative process of O_2 consumption *controls* the phosphorylative of ATP synthesis, not vice versa (see Fig. V-8). It is reiterated that a *direct kinetic and thermodynamic correlation between electron flow, O_2 consumption and ATP synthesis only occurs during the first and elusive period of the polyphasic process of oxidative phosphorylation* (see Fig. V-7). After this phase, there is neither kinetic nor thermodynamic correlation between electron flow and ATP synthesis. Indeed, the rates of all, electron flow, O_2 consumption and ATP synthesis are greatly reduced by the impairing concentrations of O_2 and O_2-radicals.

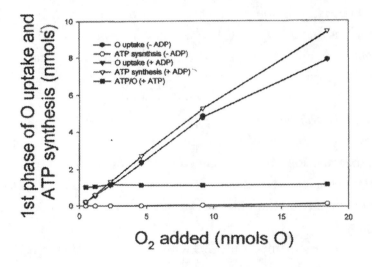

Figure V-8. The concentration of ADP and the consequent process of ATP synthesis have no effect on the extent and rates of O_2 consumption.

Under normal physiological conditions, the amount of O_2 directly involved in the process of ATP synthesis is the exclusive function of the first phase of O_2 consumption. The ATP/O stoichiometry, or the number of molecules of ATP formed per atom of O_2 reduced to water, depends on both the amount of O_2 consumed during the *first phase* of the respiratory process and the initial concentration of ADP.

KINETICS AND THERMODYNAMICS OF OXYGEN CONSUMPTION

VI. 1. Introduction

The respiratory process of O_2 consumption that occurs in aerobic cells depends on the relationship between all, enzymes [E], respiratory substrates [S], enzyme-substrate complexes [ES], product [P] and individual rate constants (k_1 to k_3), as shown below.

$$E + S \underset{k_2}{\overset{k_1}{\rightleftharpoons}} ES \overset{k_3}{\longrightarrow} E + P$$

In this diagram, [E] represents the concentration of enzymes contained in the respiratory chain and its vicinity, [S] represents the concentration respiratory substrates, including electrons, H^+ and O_2, [ES] is the complex between the free enzyme and its substrates, particularly cytochrome aa_3, H^+, electrons and O_2. Considering that the complex between the product [P] and the free enzyme (cytochrome aa_3) dos not exists, the rate constant k_4 is not represented (see above)

The ultimate limit in the rates of O_2 consumption depends on the rate of formation of the ES complex and the ratio between the rate constant k_3 and the K_M of cytochrome aa_3 for O_2 which is set by the

87

value of k_1. *This rate constant, however, cannot be faster than the diffusion controlled encounter of cytochrome aa$_3$ and its substrates* (H$^+$, electrons and O$_2$) which cannot be higher than 10^8 to 10^9 M^{-1} s^{-1}. Maximal rates of reaction (V_{max}) take place when the relationship between substrate concentration [S] and the sum of [S] and K_M is close to 1.0.

$$[O_2] / [O_2] + K_M = 1.0$$

VI. 2. The K$_M$ of Cytochrome Oxidase for Oxygen is close to 30 µM

Since 1956, when Britton Chance described the metabolic states of mitochondria, it is firmly believed that the Michaelis-Menten constant (K_M) of cytochrome oxidase for O$_2$ is between 0.05 and 0.5 µM. These values, however, were determined at the end of reactions initiated in the presence of 230 µM O$_2$ under conditions in which the rates of reaction are greatly reduced by the abnormally high levels of O$_2$ and impairing oxygen radicals. True dependence of rates O$_2$ uptake on O$_2$ concentration can only be determined under *strict first-order kinetics* when, resembling oxygen-pulse experiments, the hyperbolical rates of O$_2$ uptake are determining ms after the binding of O$_2$ to fully reduced cytochrome aa$_3$. Indeed, true rates of O$_2$ consumption are exquisitely modified by a multitude of factor, particularly by the relative concentrations of O$_2$ and cytochrome aa$_3$. Under normal physiological conditions the concentrations of O$_2$ inside the mitochondria is never higher than 70 µM. If the K_M of cytochrome aa$_3$ for O$_2$ were as low as currently believed (0.05 to 0.5 µM), maximal rates (V_{max}) of O$_2$ consumption were readily attained at any O$_2$ concentration above 5.0 µM (see Table VI-1). In reality, the K_M of cytochrome aa$_3$ for O$_2$, i.e. the concentration of O$_2$ required for *half maximal rates* of O$_2$ consumption is close to 30 µM, i.e. from 60 to 600 times higher than the range of values from 0.05 to 0.5 µM

Table VI-1

Correlation between O_2 concentration and rates of O_2 consumption

O_2 added (nmoles O)	Liver homogenates	Sub-mitochondrial particles
	μmol min^{-1} mg^{-1} protein)	
0.23	3.509	
0.575	8.475	
1.15	16.667	
2.00		6.02
2.30	32.258	
2.50		7.41
4.6	58.824	
5.0		13.69
7.5		19.61
9.2	83.333	
10.0		24.39
20.0		38.46

Source: Reynafarje, B.D., and Ferreira, *Int. J. Med. Sci.* (2008), **5(3)**, 143-151. Reactions were catalyzed by both, 10 mg of protein from homogenates of Pig liver or 0.1 mg of protein from inverted submitochondrial vesicles (SMP) of the same liver, in the presence of 5 mM NADH and 10 mM succinate.

Double reciprocal plots of data presented in Table VI-1 and Fig. VI-2, clearly demonstrate that, regardless of ΔE_h and protein (cytochrome aa_3) concentration, the K_M of cytochrome oxidase for oxygen is a constant equal to ~30 μM. Distinctly, *maximal rates of O_2 consumption* vary sensitively depending on ΔE_h and the relative concentrations of O_2 and cytochrome aa_3. In fact, even in the presence of 20 μM O_2, the rates of O_2 consumption are orders of magnitude higher than under state-3 metabolic conditions in the presence of 230 μM O_2 (see Fig. VI-1)

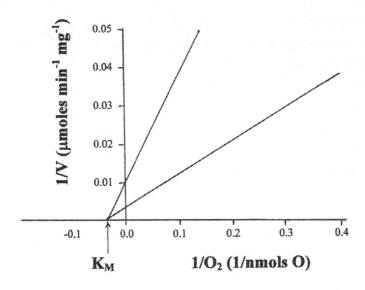

Figure VI-1. The Lineweaver-Burk plot of data presented in Table VI-1 demonstrates that the K_M of cytochrome aa_3 for O_2 is constant while the *maximal rates* of O_2 consumption vary depending on the relative concentrations of O_2 and cytochrome aa_3.

VI. 3. Effect of the O/cytochrome aa$_3$ ratio on the extent of O$_2$ consumption

The consensus is that, regardless of the concentration of cytochrome aa_3, the stoichiometries between electron flow and O_2 uptake ($2e^-/O$ ratio), H^+ *ejection* and O_2 uptake (H^+/O ratio), and ATP synthesis and O_2 uptake (ATP/O ratio) are constants that only depend on the redox potential (ΔE_h). Thus, to this day it is believed that the $2e^-/O$ ratio for NADH oxidation is ~10, and that the ATP/O ratios for the oxidation of NADH, succinate and cytochrome c are respectively close to 3.0, 2.0 and 1.5. Under *in vivo* conditions, however, a strict kinetic and thermodynamic correlation between net flow of electrons, O_2 and H^+ uptake and ATP synthesis only occurs during the hyperbolical process of O_2 consumption in which cytochrome aa_3 undergoes net oxidation. In fact, the actual process of ATP synthesis takes place during the first milliseconds of the respiratory process that was generally considered to be an "experimental artifact" (see figure V-7). Data in Table VI-2 show the intricate type of correlation that exists between the relative concentrations of O_2 and cytochrome aa_3 and the extents of O_2 and H^+ uptake that occur during the 1st phase of O_2 consumption that is directly related to the process of ATP synthesis.

Table VI-2. Correlation between the O_2 / cytochrome aa_3 ratio
and the extents of O_2 and H^+ uptake during the
first phase of the respiratory process

O / cytochrome (ratio)	O consumed in 1st phase (nmols O)	%	H^+ uptake	H^+/O
2.5	2.25	90	4.50	2.0
5.0	3.80	76	7.60	2.0
10	5.80	58	11.60	2.0
15	6.30	42	12.60	2.0
20	6.40	32	12.80	2.0
25	6.30	25	12.60	2.0
30	6.00	20	12.00	2.0
40	3.60	9	7.20	2.0
50	1.50	3	3.00	2.0
70	0.6	0.9	1.20	2.0

During the sigmoidal process of ATP synthesis, the extremely fast and hyperbolical processes of electron flow, O_2 consumption, H^+ uptake, and net oxidation of *cytochrome aa_3* are an intricate function of the relative concentrations of O_2 and *cytochrome aa_3*. However, regardless of the actual concentrations of O_2 and *cytochrome aa_3* the H^+/O uptake ratio is always 2.0 and equal to the stoichiometry of O_2 reduction to water.

Data in Table VI-2 show that, although the *percent* of O_2 consumed in the 1st phase is inversely related to the amount of O_2 consumption, the *maximal amount* of O_2 consumed during the synthesis of ATP only occurs in a narrow range of O_2/*cytochrome aa_3* ratios. Figure VI-2 shows that the extent of O_2 consumption and the consequent synthesis of ATP are greatly reduced when the O/cytochrome aa_3 ratio is either lower of higher than 20.

At any O_2/cytochrome aa_3 ratios *lower* than 10 the extents of O_2 consumption, H^+ uptake and ATP synthesis are greatly reduced, most likely due to a deficiency in O_2 concentration. At any O_2/cytochrome aa_3 ratio higher than 10 the extents of O_2 consumption and ATP synthesis are, in all probability, reduced due to the impairing effects of an excess of O_2 and oxygen-radicals. Keep in mind that under normal physiological conditions the maximal concentration of O_2 inside the cell is no higher than 70 µM.

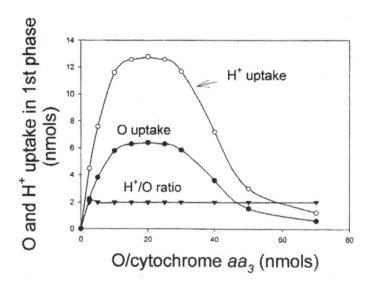

Figure VI-2. Correlation between the O_2/cytochrome aa_3 ratio and the extents of O_2 and H^+ uptake.

VI. 4. The vectorial ejection of H⁺ has no effect on the process of ATP synthesis

Ever since Mitchell formulated his chemiosmotic hypothesis, it is firmly believed that the main source of energy required for the synthesis of ATP is a protonmotive force (Δp) of 5.2 kcal per mole of vectorial H^+ ejected during the respiratory process of O_2 consumption. Thus, to this day the consensus amongst researches is that the H^+/O ratio of NADH oxidation is 10 and that the consequent H^+/ATP stoichiometry of ATP synthesis is 4.0. These values, however, were obtained in oxygen-pulse experiments in which the extents of H^+ *ejection* were determined far away from the elusive and extremely fast process of O_2 consumption during which the synthesis of ATP takes place. In reality, *the vectorial ejection of H⁺ follows the extremely fast and hyperbolical processes of O_2 consumption and cytochrome aa_3 oxidation and the sigmoidal process of ATP synthesis.* The net ejection of H^+ coincides with the slow phase of O_2 consumption (classic state-4 metabolic conditions) and the reduction, rather than the oxidation, of cytochrome aa_3 (Fig. VI-3)

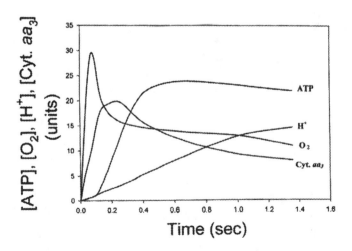

Figure VI-3. Time course of the processes of O_2 uptake, H^+ ejection, ATP synthesis, and cytochrome *aa₃* oxidation [After Reynafarje & Ferreira Int. J. Med. Sci. (2008): 5:147]

Regardless of the *extent* and rates of O_2 consumption and ATP synthesis, the *ejection of H^+* coincides with the ensuing slow phase of O_2 consumption, the *reduction* (not the oxidation) of cytochrome aa_3, and the *hydrolysis* rather than synthesis of ATP. Entirely different than the process of H^+ uptake, which is independent of the extent and redox-state of cytochrome aa_3, the ejection of vectorial *H^+ is the exclusive function of the concentration of cytochrome aa_3*, always occurring with a stoichiometry of nearly 12 (see Table VI-3 and figure VI- 4).

Table VI-3. Extent of H^+ ejection by *cytochrome aa_3* embedded in liposomes.

Cytochrome aa_3. (nmols)	O / cytochrome aa_3 (ratio)	H^+ ejection (nmols)	H^+/ O ejection (ratio)	H+/Cytochrome aa_3
0.20	250.0	2.4	0.06	12.0
0.60	62.5	7.2	0.19	12.0
1.20	30.0	14.4	0.39	12.0
2.30	15.9	27.6	0.75	12.0

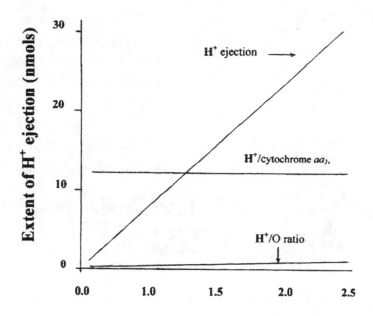

Figure VI-4. Relationship between the extents of H⁺ ejection
and cytochrome aa_3

Regardless of the relative concentrations of O_2 and cytochrome aa_3 the H⁺/O ejection-ratio is always significantly below 1.0.

KINETICS AND THERMODYNAMICS OF ATP SYNTHESIS

VII. 1. Introduction

Shortly after the discovery of oxygen, Lavoisier demonstrated that the process of O_2 consumption was associated with the production of essential forms of energy. One of the most important forms of this energy is ATP, which is the universal currency of free energy in living organisms. Close to 95% of the energy generated by the cell at the mitochondrial level is in the form of ATP. The exact mechanism by which ATP is synthesized is, however, not yet entirely understood. In accordance with the chemiosmotic hypothesis of Mitchell the consensus is that the protonmotive force (Δp), generated during the respiratory process of O_2 consumption, is the most fundamental form of free energy involved in the actual process of ATP synthesis.

Recently, however, it was unequivocally demonstrated that, under *in vivo* concentrations of O_2 (near zero to ~60 µM), the net synthesis of ATP can take place in the absolute absence of Δp, exclusively depending on the free energy of electron transport. In fact, whether the oxidative phosphorylation process is catalyzed by whole cells, intact mitochondria or frozen/thawed vesicles of SMP, the net synthesis of

ATP depends on the free energy of electrons flow and O_2 reduction to water (see Figs. V -7, VI- 4 and VII-3).

VII. 2. The synthesis of ATP depends more on O_2 than on ADP concentration

It is currently believed that the most important form of free energy involved in the process of ATP synthesis is the protonmotive force (Δp), and that *"electrons do not flow from fuel molecules to O_2 unless ADP is simultaneously phosphorylated to ATP"*. In other words, *the levels of ADP and the process of ATP synthesis control the respiratory processes of electron flow and oxygen reduction to water.* On the contrary, it was unequivocally demonstrated that the exergonic processes of electron flow from a reduced respiratory substrate to O_2 control the level of ADP and the endergonic process of ATP synthesis not *vice versa* (see section V and Fig. V-8). The following facts confirm this assertion.

First, regardless of redox potential (ΔE_h) and ADP concentration, the *actual rates of ATP synthesis* are orders of magnitude higher under *in vivo* levels of O_2 (near zero to 70 µM) than under classic state-3 metabolic conditions in the presence of ~230 µM O_2 (see Fig. VII-1).

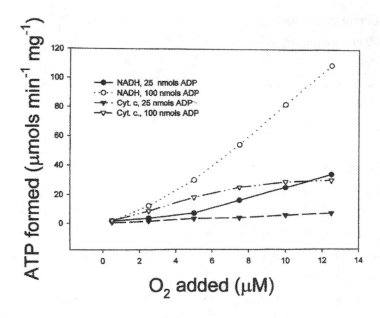

Figure VII-1. Rates of ATP synthesis in reactions catalyzed by 0.15 mg protein of RLM depend more on the initial concentration of O_2 than on the levels of ADP and ΔE_h [After Reynafarje & Ferreira Int. J. Med. Sci. (2008), 5(3):143-151]

It is mechanistically significant that at low *in vivo* levels of O_2 (near zero to 12 µM) the rates of ATP synthesis are higher in the presence of cytochrome *c* and high levels of ADP than in the presence of NADH and low levels of ADP, i.e. higher at low than at a high ΔE_h. Obviously, at very low levels of O_2 the rates of ATP synthesis depend more on the concentration of ADP than on the ΔE_h. Only at O_2 concentrations higher than 12 µM the rates of ATP synthesis depend more on the ΔE_h than on the level of ADP. Furthermore, data depicted in Figure VII-2 unequivocally demonstrate that not only the rates but also the *extents* of ATP synthesis depend more sensitively on the initial concentration of O_2 than on the ΔE_h and the actual concentration of ADP. To this day, however, it is still believed that the ATP/O stoichiometry is constant, the value of which only depends on the magnitude of the ΔE_h. Thus, the ATP/O ratio for the oxidation of cytochrome c, succinate and NADH is considered to be equal to 1.5, 2.0 and 3.0, respectively.

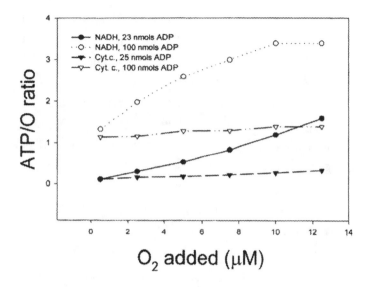

Figure VII-2. Dependence of the ATP/O stoichiometry on the ΔE_h and the levels of O_2 and ADP [Data taken from Reynafarje & Ferreira in Int. J. Med. Sci. 2008, 5(3):143-151]

In reality, the ATP/O stoichiometry is not constant but normally changes from near zero to 3.4 intricately depending on all, the ΔE_h and the relative concentrations of ADP, O_2 and cytochrome aa_3 (Fig. VII-2). It is mechanistically significant that in the presence of very low levels of O_2 and high of ADP the ATP/O ratio can be up to 10 times higher in the presence of cytochrome c alone than in the presence of NADH and low levels of ADP. Only at high levels of both O_2 and ADP the ATP/O stoichiometry attains values that are higher in the presence of NADH than in the presence of cytochrome c alone.

Considering that the ATP/O ratio of NADH oxidation is constantly 3.0 the impressive assertion has been made that the "cell energy cycle may turn over at rest as much as half and adult's weight in ATP per day, and many times more during *physical exercise* or work". If this assertion were true the efficiency of the cell to synthesize ATP would be abnormally low.

Obviously, under *absolute resting conditions*, when the expenditure of free energy is minimal and the cytochrome aa_3 is mostly oxidized (deficient in electrons and protons) the ATP/O stoichiometry is reduced to near zero or just enough to maintain the homeostasis of the cell. Conversely, after an abrupt and *intense physical exercise*, when the mitochondria are fully reduced and charged with ADP, the ATP/O ratio attains maximal values the instant in *which* O_2 diffuses from cytosol to matrix driven by a large gradient of O_2 concentrations.

VII. 3. The efficiency of the mitochondrial process of ATP synthesis

Knowing that the ΔGp of ATP synthesis is equal to the difference between the ratio of concentrations of substrates and products at the beginning and equilibrium, the efficiency of ATP synthesis can be evaluated in coupled reactions by using the following equation.

$$\Delta Gp = RT\, ln\, [ATP]^{\,a} [S]^{\,b} / [ADP]^{\,c} [Pi]^{\,d} [O_2]^{\,e} [SH_2]^{\,f} - RT\, ln\, K_{eq},$$

where R is the gas constant (1.987 cal x mole^{-1} x $^{\circ}$K^{-1}), T is the absolute temperature ($^{\circ}$K), S and SH$_2$ are, respectively, the oxidized and reduced forms of respiratory substrates (NADH, succinate, cytochrome c) and K_{eq} is the equilibrium constant. The coefficients of ATP, S, ADP, Pi, O$_2$ and SH$_2$ are respectively represented by $a, b, c, d, and f.$

Thus, more than half a century ago, Lehninger showed that mitochondria made permeable to ions and metabolites by water treatment are able to synthesize ATP with high efficiency. In fact we have unambiguously demonstrated that, even in the absence of a proton gradient, frozen/thawed samples of inverted-inner membrane vesicles can synthesize ATP with an efficiency of nearly 100% (see Fig. VII-3). Considering that the maximal ATP/O ratio is 3.4, the

ΔGp of ATP synthesis is 15.1 kcal/mol, and the free energy of ATP synthesis at equilibrium is -52.6 kcal /mole, it is was calculated that the *efficiency of ATP synthesis* (15.1 x 3.4/52.6 = 98) is close to 100%.

Data presented in Fig. VII-3 shows that, regardless of ΔE_h, ADP and O_2 concentration, the mot important factors in determining the magnitude of ΔGp are the relative concentrations of O_2 and protein, i.e. the O_2 per cytochrome aa_3 ratio (see Fig. VI-2). At the same ΔE_h (oxidation of NADH) and ADP concentration the efficiency in the generation of ΔGp is greatly reduced when the O_2 per protein ration is greatly reduced, as it is shown in Fig. VI-2.

Obviously the concentrations of O_2 and degree of reduction of cytochrome aa_3 play fundamental roles in the endergonic process of ATP synthesis.

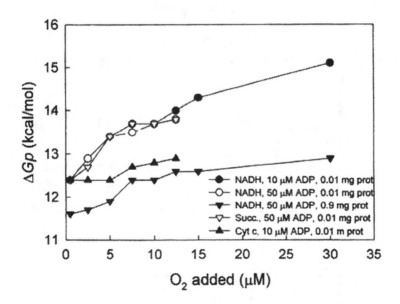

Figure VII-3. The ΔGp, in reactions catalyzed by inverted inner membrane vesicles, depend more on the relative concentrations of O_2 and cytochrome aa_3 than on the level of ΔE_h and the concentration of ADP.

Confirming data presented in Figs. VII-1 and VII-2, data in Fig. VII-3 show that, regardless of ΔE_h and ADP concentration, the magnitude of ΔGp is directly related to the extent and degree of reduction of cytochrome aa_3. Only in a very small range of O_2 per cytochrome aa_3 ratios the free energy of electron flow is kinetically and thermodynamically related to the oxidative phosphorylation process of ATP synthesis. It is reiterated that the synthesis of ATP only occurs during the respiratory process of O_2 consumption in which cytochrome aa_3 undergoes net oxidation.

VII. 4. Net synthesis of ATP takes place in the absence of a protonmotive force

In accordance with the chemiosmotic hypothesis of Mitchell the consensus is that the most fundamental source of free energy involved in the phosphorylative process of ATP synthesis from ADP and P_i is the protonmotive force (Δp). Thus, the electrical (E_m) and chemical (ΔpH^+) components of Δp contribute to the endergonic process of ATP synthesis in the following manner.

$$\Delta p = E_m - 2.303\ RT/F \times \Delta pH = E_m - 0.06\ \Delta pH \qquad (1)$$

where E_m is equal to 0.14 V, R is the gas constant equal to 1.987 cal x mole^{-1}, T is the absolute temperature (298° K at 25° C), F is the Faraday equal to 23,060 V^{-1} and the value of ΔpH is -1.4 units, lower in the cytosol than in the matrix, i.e.

$$\Delta p = 0.14\ V - 2.303 \times 1.987 \times 298/23,060\ cal\ V^{-1} \times \Delta pH = -0.06\ \Delta pH,$$

or

$$\Delta p = 0.14\ V - 0.059\ V \times -1.4 = 0.14\ V + 0.083 = 0.223\ V \qquad (2)$$

The total proton-motive force of 0.223 V corresponds to a standard free energy change, $\Delta G°$, of only 5.2 kcal/mole, from which 63% is in the form of the electrical potential (E_m) and 37% in the form of a proton gradient. In reality, however, the most fundamental form of energy involved in the process of ATP synthesis comes not from the Δp but from the flow of electrons from NADH or $FADH_2$ to O_2.

The standard reduction potential, $\Delta E'_0$, derived from the oxidation of NADH is the difference between the half reactions of O_2 to water and NAD^+,

$$\tfrac{1}{2}\,O_2 + 2\,H^+ + 2\,e^+ = H_2O \qquad \Delta E'_0 = +0.82\ V \qquad (3)$$
$$NAD^+ + H^+ + 2\,e^+ = NADH \qquad \Delta E'_0 = -0.32\ V \qquad (4)$$

Subtracting equation (4) from equation (3) yields

$$\tfrac{1}{2}\,O_2 + NADH + H^+ = H_2O + NAD^+ \qquad \Delta E'_0 = +1.14\ V \qquad (5)$$

This equation indicates that "a potential difference of 1.14 volts drives the flow of electrons from NADH to O_2 with the following standard free energy change:

$$\Delta G^{o'} = -nF\Delta E'_0 = -2 \times 23.060\ kcal\ V^{-1} \times 1.14\ V = -52.6\ kcal/mol \qquad (6)$$

Since the ΔpH component of the Δp is no more than 0.083 V, i.e. only 7.37% of the energy released during the oxidation of NADH (1.14 V), it is evident that the sole gradient of protons is not enough to guaranty an efficient process of ATP synthesis.

Current experimental evidence indicates that, during the synthesis of ATP, the terminal atom of O_2 in the molecule of ADP attracts a phosphorous atom to form a penta covalent intermediate, which then dissociates into ATP and H_2O.

Paul Boyer proposed that *the role of the proton gradient is not to form ATP but to release it from the ATP synthase.* He found that the nucleotide-binding sites of this enzyme interact with each other and that the enzyme exhibits *catalytic cooperativity.* In order words, the binding of ADP and P_i to one site promotes the release of ATP from another, and that *ATP does not leave the catalytic site unless protons flow through the enzyme.*

In accordance with this idea, it is assumed that chloroplasts, with a CF_0-CF_1 synthase similar to the F_0-F_1 synthase of mitochondria, synthesize ATP in the absence of electron flow, only using the driving force of a pH gradient of near 4 units. It is quite possible, however, that the extremely large gradient of protons imposed to the thylakoid membrane induces conformational changes similar to those induced by the flow of electrons during the respiratory process of electron flow at the mitochondrial level. In fact, there is now undeniable experimental evidence that the oxidative phosphorylation process of ATP synthesis, which in the presence of *in vivo* levels of O_2 occurs with maximal efficiency, takes place in the absolute absence of a proton gradient, ΔpH, (see Fig. VII-3).

VII. 5. Distinct mechanisms for the synthesis and hydrolysis of ATP

Because the synthesis and hydrolysis of ATP are catalyzed by the same enzyme, it is still believed that the mechanisms by which these two processes take place are the same. Under *in vivo* concentrations of O_2 and normal physiological conditions, however, the mechanisms of ATP synthesis and ATP hydrolysis are entirely different. The experimentally determined facts provide undeniable evidence that the mechanisms of ATP synthesis and ATP hydrolysis have the following essential characteristics.

First, the process of oxidative phosphorylation is *polyphasic in nature* and a strict kinetic and thermodynamic correlation between O_2

uptake and ATP synthesis only occurs during the extremely fast and elusive process in which cytochrome aa_3 undergoes net oxidation

Second, the respiratory processes of electron flow and O_2 consumption *precede, rather than follow,* the phosphorylative process of ATP synthesis (see Fig. V-7). Contrary to the textbook statements that *"electrons do not flow from fuel molecules to O_2 unless ADP is simultaneously phosphorylated to ATP"*, the *processes electron flow and oxygen consumption "control" the level of ADP and the process of ATP synthesis.* In fact, the initially *hyperbolical* processes of electron flow and O_2 consumption provide a much more sensitive control of the level of ADP and the *sigmoidal process of ATP synthesis.* Only when the mitochondrial level of O_2 has decreased to near zero, and the cytochrome aa_3 is fully reduced, the synthesis of ATP occurs at maximal rates the instant in which O_2 diffuses from cytosol to matrix driven by a very high gradient of O_2 concentrations.

Third, the catalytic sites of the F_1 moiety hydrolyze ATP in a kinetically equivalent manner, i.e. the binding of ATP to one site has no effect on the intrinsic dissociation constants of the vacant sites and the overall process of ATP hydrolysis yields a normal *hyperbolical curve.* Distinctly, the catalytic sites of the F_1 moiety synthesize ATP in a *cooperative manner* so that the binding of ADP to a catalytic site increases the activity of adjacent vacant sites in such a way that the overall time-course of ATP synthesis is *sigmoidal* in nature. The potential advantage of the *sigmoidal process of ATP synthesis over the hyperbolical of ATP hydrolysis* is that the latter only occurs at the end of the initial phase of O_2 consumption when the extent of ATP synthesis is maximal and the extent of ADP minimal.

Fourth, the K_M of cytochrome aa_3 for O_2, i.e. the concentration of O_2 required for half maximal rates of O_2 consumption and ATP synthesis is close to 30 µM; 60 to 600 times higher than the currently accepted values from 0.5 to 0.05 µM. These extremely low values, however, were determined at the end or reactions initiated in the presence of ~230 µM O_2 when the process of O_2 consumption does not exclusively depend on O_2 concentration and the rates of O_2 consumption do not obey *true first-order kinetics*. Only during the first and elusive phase of the respiratory process (see Fig. V-7) the rates of O_2 consumption strictly depend on O_2 concentration. If the K_M of cytochrome aa_3 for O_2 were bellow 0.5 µM, as generally assumed, maximal rates of O_2 consumption were readily obtained at any O_2 concentrations higher than 10 µM O_2. In reality, the *rates* of O_2 consumption that occur under in vivo levels of O_2 (near zero to 70 µM), are orders of magnitude higher than those observed under classic state-3 metabolic conditions in the presence of ~230 µM O_2 (see Fig. VII-1).

Fifth, the ATP/O stoichiometry or number of molecules of ATP formed per atom of O_2 reduced to water is not constant (see Fig. VII-1) but change from near zero to 3.4 intricately depending on the ΔE_h, the concentration of ADP and relative concentrations of O_2 and cytochrome aa_3. Thus, under absolute resting conditions, when the concentration of O_2 in the matrix is *maximal* and the inner mitochondrial membrane is mostly oxidized, the ATP/O ratio is *minimal* and just enough to maintain the homeostasis of the cell. Entirely different, under conditions of abrupt physical exercise, when the concentration of O_2 inside the cell is *minimal* and the inner mitochondrial membrane is fully reduced, the ATP/O ratio attains *maximal values* the instant in which O_2 is once more made available. If the ATP/O ratio, in the presence of NADH, were constantly 3.0, the efficiency of the energy cycle of the cell to generate ATP would be abnormally low.

Sixth, the ejection of vectorial H^+ is neither kinetically nor stoichiometrically related to the process of ATP *synthesis. Net ejection of vectorial H^+* only occurs during the respiratory process that follows all, net flow of electrons, hyperbolical phase of O_2 consumption, net oxidation of cytochrome aa_3, and *net synthesis of ATP* (see Fig. VI-4).

Finally and most important, *the respiratory processes of electron flow and O_2 reduction provide the free energy involved in the actual process of ATP synthesis by inducing structural and conformational changes at the levels of the cytochrome aa_3 and ATP synthase.* In all probability, the γ subunit of the ATP synthase rotates in opposite directions during the the synthesis and hydrolysis of ATP as shown in figure VII-4. During the uphill and *endergonic process of ATP synthesis* the free energy of electron flow along the cytochrome aa_3 rotates the γ subunit in a counter-clockwise direction that is in tightly connected with the β subunit of the ATP-synthase. On the contrary, during the downhill and *exergonic process of ATP hydrolysis,* the γ subunit of the ATP-synthase *freely rotates in a clockwise direction* without changing the specific affinity of the β subunits for its substrate ATP

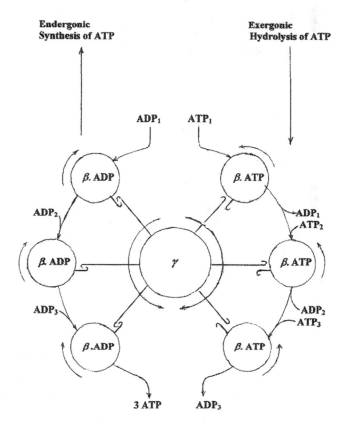

Figure VII- 4. Diagrammatic representation of the reverse rotation of the γ and β subunit of the ATP-synthase during the processes of ATP synthesis of ATP hydrolysis

REFERENCES

Books:

Caughey, W.S. (ed.), 1979. Biochemical and Clinical Aspects of Oxygen Academic Press New York London Toronto Sydney San Francisco

Cramer, W.A. and Knaff, D.B., 1989. *Energy Transduction in Biological Membranes* Springer-Verlag. New York

Ernster, L. (ed.), 1992. *Molecular Mechanisms in Bioenergetics*. Elsevier

Ganong, W.F., 1993. *Review of Medical Physiology* (16th edition) Appleton & Lange.

Lehninger, A.L., 1978. *Bioquimica* (1st edition) Ediciones Omega, S.A. Casanova, 220, Barcelona-11

Lahiri, S., Forster, R.E., II, Davies, R.O., Pack, A.I. 1989. *Chemoreceptors and Reflexes In Breathing*: *Cellular and Molecular Aspects* (eds.) New York Oxford, Oxford University Press

Helfferich, C. (ed.), 1996. *The Physiology of Work in Cold and Altitude.* Arctic Aeromedical Laboratory FT. Wainwright, Alaska.

Mitchell, P. (1968). "Chemiosmotic Coupling and Energy Transduction". Glynn Research, Bodmin, Cornwall, U.K.

Nicholls, D. 1982. *Bioenergetics* (1st edition) Academic Press. London New York

Nicholls, D.G., and Ferguson, S.J. 1992. *Bioenergetics* 2. Academic Press Nework

Segel, I. H. 1968. *Biochemical Calculations* (2nd edition). John Wiley & Sons, New York. Chichester. Brisbane. Toronto

Stryer, L., 1996. *Biochemistry* (3rd edition) W.H. Freeman and Company New York Articles:

Abrahams, J.P., Leslie, A.G.W., Lutter, R., and Walker, J.E. (1994). *Nature (London)* 370:621-628

Akerman, K.E.O. and Wikstrom, M.K.F. (1976) *FEBS Lett.* 68:191-197.

Bianchet, M.A., Pedersen, P.L., and Amzel, L.M. (2000) *J. Bioenerg. Biomemb.* 32: 517-521

Bockmann, R.A. Grubmuller, H. (2002) *Nat Struct Biol.* 9(3):198-202

Boyer, P.D., Cross, R.L. and Momsen, W. (1973) *Proc. Natl. Acad. Sci. USA* 70:2837-2839

Boyer, P.D. (1981). *Annu. Rev. Biochem.* 66, 717-749

Boyer, P.D (1993) *Biochim. Biophys. Acta* 1140:215-250

Boyer, P.D. (1993) *Biochim. Biophys, Acta* 1140:215-250

Boyer, P.D. (2002) *J. Biol. Chem.* 277:39045-39061

Brand, M.D., Reynafarje, B. and Lehinger, A.L. (1976) *Proc. Natl. Acad. Sci. USA* 73:437-441

Brand, M.D., Reynafarje, B. and Lehninger, A.L. (1976) *J. Biol. Chem.* 251: 5670-5676

Brand, M.D. (1977) *Biochem. Soc. Trans.* 5:1615-1620

Brand, M.D. and Murphy, M.P. (1987) *Biol. Rev.* 62: 41-193

Brand, M.D. (1994) *The Biochemist.* 16:20-24

Brzezinski, P. and Adelroth, P. (1998) *J. Bioenerg. Biomembr.* 30: 99-107

Chance, B. and Williams, G.R. (1955) *J. Biol. Chem.* 217:383-393.

Chance, B. and Williams, G.R. (1955) *J. Biol. Chem.* 217:395-407.

Chance, B. and Williams, G.R. (1955) *J. Biol. Chem.* 217:409-427.

Chance, B. and Williams, G.R. (1955) *J. Biol. Chem.* 217:439-451.

Chance, B. and Williams, G.R. (1956) *J. Biol. Chem.* 221:447-489.

Chance, B. and Williams, G.R. (1956) *J. Biol. Chem.* 221:447-489

Chance, B. and Williams, G.R. (1956) *Advances in Enzymology.* Interscience Publishers Ltd., London.

Chance, B. (1965) *J. Gen. Physiol.* 49:163-188.

Chance, B., Leigh, J.S. Jr., Kent, J., McCully, K., Nioka, S., Clark, B.J., Maris, J.M. and Graham, T. (1986) *Proc. Natl. Acad. Sci.* 83:9458-9462

Costa, L.W., Reynafarje, B. and Lehninger, A.L. (1984) *J. Biol. Chem.* 259:4802-4811

Davies, P.W. (1962) In: *Physiological Techniques in Biological Research.* W.L. Nastuk N.Y. 4:137-179

Drose, S. and Brandt, U. ((2008) *J. Biol. Chem.* 283:21649-21654

Erecinska, M. and Wilson, D.F. (1978) *Arch. Biochem. Biophys.* 188:1-14

Erecinska, M. and Wilson, D.F. (1978) *J. Membrane Biol.* 70:1-14

Ferguson, S.J. (1986) *Trends Biochem. Sci.* 11:351-353

Ferreira, J., Reynafarje, B., Costa, L.E. and Lehninger, A.L. (1988) *Cancer Research* 48:628-634

Fillingame, R.H. (1992) *J. Bioenerg. Biomemb.* 24:485-491

Fillingame, R.H. (1992) *J. Bioenerg. Biomemb.* 24:485-491

Fujikawa, M., Imamura, H., Nakamura, J. and Yoshida, M. (2012)) *J. Biol. Chem.* 287:18781-18787

Greenwood, C. and Gibson, Q.H. (1967) *J. Biol. Chem.* 242:1782-1787

Herweijer, M.A., Berden, J.A. and Slater, E.C. (1986) *Biochim. Biophys. Acta.* 849: 276-287

Hinkle, P.C., Kumar, M.A., Recetar, A. and Harris, D.L. (1991) *Biochemistry* 30:3576-3682

Hill, B.C. (1984) *Biochem. J.* 218:913-921

Hill, B.C. (1991) *J. Biol. Chem.* 266:2219-2226

Jancura, D.Berka, V., Antalik, M, Bagelova, J, Gennis, R.B., Palmer, G. and Fabian, M. (2006) *J. Biol. Chem.* 281:30319-30325

Kaim, G. and Dimroth, P. (1997) *The EMBO J.* 18:4118-4127

Kannt, A., Roy, C., Lancaster, D. and Michel, H. (1998) *J. Bioenerg. Biomembr.* 30:81-87

Lehninger, A.L. (1979) in "Hormones and Energy Metabolism". Klachko, D.M.Anderson, R.R. and Heimbaerg M. (eds.). *Some Aspects of Energy Coupling by Mitochondria*, 1-16.

Lehninger, A.L., Reynafarje, B., Hendler, R.W., Shrager, R.I. *FEBS Letters* 192:173-178

Lemasters, J.J., Grunwald, R. and Emaus, R.K. (1984) *J. Biol. Chem.* 259:3058-3063

Lemasters, J.J. and Billica, W.H. (1981) *J. Biol. Chem.* 256:12949-12957

Leyva, J.A., Bianchet, M.A. and Amzel, L.M. (2003) *Mol. Membr. Biol.* 20:27-33

Luft, R. (1994) *Proc. Natl. Acad. Sci, USA* 91:8731-8738

Matsuno-Yagi, A. and Hatefi, Y. (1985) *J. Biol. Chem.* 260:14424-14427

Matsuno-Yagi, A. and Hatefi, Y. (1990) *J. Biol. Chem.* 265:82-88

Matsuno-Yagi, A. and Hatefi, Y. (1993) *J. Biol. Chem.* 268:1539-1545

Menz, I.I., Walker, J.E. and Leslie, A.G.W. (2001) *Cell* 106:331-141

Mitchell, P. (1961) *Nature (London)* 191:423-427

Mitchell, P. and Moyle, J. (1965) *Nature (London)* 208:147-151

Mitchell, P. and Moyle, J. (1967) *Biochem. J.* 105:1147-1162

Mitchell, P., Mitchell, R., Moody, A.J., West, I.C., Baum, H. and Wrigglesworth, J.M. (1985) *FEBS LETTERS* 188:1-7

Mnatsakanyan,N., Hook, J.A., Quisenberry, L. and Weber, J. (2009) *J. Biol. Chem.* 284:26519-26525

Nakamoto, R.K., Ketchum, C.J., Kuo, P.H. Peskova, Y.B. and Al-Shawi, M.K. (2000) *Biochim. Biophys. Acta.* 1458(2-3): 289-299

Nakano, M. Imamura, H. Toei, M. Tamakoshi, M. Yoshida, M. and Yokoyama, K. (2008) *J. Biol. Chem.* 283:20789-20796

Pedersen, P.L and Amzel, L.M. (1993) *J. Biol. Chem.* 268:9937-9940

Penefsky, H.S., and Cross, R.L. (11991) *Advan. Enzymol. Mol. Biol.* 64:173-214

Penniston, J.T. (1973) *Biochemistry* 12:650-654

Perez, J.A. and Ferguson, S.J. (1990) *Biochemistry* 29:10503-10518

Perez, J.A. and Ferguson, S.J. (1990) *Biochemistry* 129:10518-10526

Reynafarje, B. and Lehninger, A.L. (1974) *J. Biol. Chem.* 249:6067-6074

Reynafarje, B., Brand, M.D. and Lehninger, A.L. (1976) *J. Biol. Chem.* 251:7442-7451

Reynafarje, B., Alexandre, A., Davies, P. And Lehninger, A.L. (1982) *Proc. Natl. Acad. Sci. USA.* 79:7218-7222

Reynafarje, B., Costa, L.E., Lehninger, A.L. (1985) *Analytial Biochem.* 145:406-418

Reynafarje, B. and Davies, P.W. (1990) *Am. J. Physiol.* 258 (Cell Physiol. 27): C506-C511

Reynafarje, B. (1991) *Biochem. Biophys. Res. Commun.* 176:150-156

Reynafarje, B. and Pedersen, P.L. (1996) *J. Biol. Chem.* 271:32546-32550

Reynafarje, B. and Ferreira, J. (2002) *J. Bioenerg. Biomembr.* 34:259-267

Reynafarje, B. and Ferreira, J. (2008) IN. J. Med. Sci. 5(3):143-151

Rosing, J., Kayalar, C. and Boyer, P.D. (1977) *J. Biol. Chem.* 252:2478-2485

Sinior, A.E. (1990) *Ann. Rev. Biophys. Chem.* 19:7-41

Slater, E.C., Berden, J.A. and Herweijer, M.A. (1985) *Biochim. Biophys. Acta.* 281: 217-231

Soga, N., Kinosita Jr., K.Yoshida, M. and Suzuki, T. (2012)) *J. Biol. Chem.* 287: 9633-9639

Sun, S.X., Wang, H. and Oster, G. (2004) *Biophysical J.* 86:1373-1384

Sunamura, Ei-Ichiro, Konno, H., Imashimizu, M., Mochimaru, M. And Hisabori, T. (2012) *J. Biol. Chem.* 287: 38695-38704

Thomas, P.J., Bianchet, M., Garboczi, D.N., Hullihen, J. Amzel, L.M. and Pedersen, P.L. (1992) *Biochim. Biophys. Acta.* 1101:228-231

Vercesi, A., Reynafarje, B. and Lehninger, A.L. (1978) *J. Biol. Chem.* 253:6379-6385

Wikstrom, M., Morgan, J.E. and Verkhovsky, M.I. (1998) *J. Bioenerg. Biomembr.* 30:139-145

Wilson, D.A., Erecinska, M., Drown, C. and Silver, I.A. (1977) *Arch. Biochem. Biophys.* 195:485-493

Wilson, D.F., Owen, C.S. and Holian, A. (1977) *Arch. Biochem. Biophys.* 182:749-762

Wittenberg, B.A. and Wittenberg, J.B. (1985) *J. Biol. Chem.* 260:6548-6554

Wikstrom, M.K.F. and Saari, H.T. (1977) *Biochim. Biophys. Acta.* 462: 347-361

PHYSICAL CONSTANTS AND CONVERSION OF UNITS

Physical constant	Symbol	Significance
Ampere	A	A unit of electric current in the meter-kilogram-second system, specified as one International coulomb per second and equal to 0.999835 ampere
Atmosphere	atm	A unit of pressure equalto the air pressure at sea level, approximately equal to 1.01325×10^5 newtons per square meter.
Atomic mass unit	$Dalton$	A unit of mass equal to 1/12 the mass of the most abundant isotope of carbon
Avogadro's number	N	The number of molecules in a mole of a substance approximately 6.0225×10^{23} mole^{-1}
Boltzmann constant	k	A constant that relates the average kinetic energy of particles in a gas to the temperature of the gas. The ideal-gas law is given by: $PV = NkT$
Calorie	cal	The quantity of heat required to raise the temperature of 1 gram of water by 1°C from a standard initial temperature (3.98°C, 14.5°C or 19.5 1°C) at 1 atmosphere pressure

Celsius	*C*	Relating to a temperature scale that registers the freezing point of water as O° and the boiling point as 100° under normal atmospheric pressure
Coulomb	*C*	The meter-kilogram-second unit of electrical charge equal to the quantity of charge transferred in one second by a steady current of one ampere
Curie	*Ci*	A unit of radioactivity, equal to the amount of a radioactive isotope that decays at the rate of 3.7×10^{10} disintegrations per second
Dyne	*dyn*	A centimeter-gram-second unit or force, equal to the force required to impart an acceleration of one centimeter per second per second to a mass of one gram.
Electron volt	*ev*	A unit of energy equal to the energy acquired by an electron falling through a potential difference of one volt, approximately 1.602×10^{-19} joule.
Faraday	*Far*	The quantity of electricity that is capable of depositing or liberating 1 gram equivalent weight of a substance in electrolysis, approximately 9.6494×10^{4} coulombs. One faraday = 23.062 kcal V^{-1} mol^{-1}
Gas constant	*R*	A constant equal to 1.987 calories per degree Celsius. The constant of proportionality in the equation: $P \times V = R \times T (K)$
Joule	*J*	The international System unit of electrical, mechanical, and thermal energy. A unit of energy equal to the work done when a force of 1 newton acts through a distance of 1 meter Kelvin *K* A unit of absolute temperature equal to 1/273.16 of the absolute temperature. This unit is equal to one Celsius degree.

Newton	N	The unit of force required to accelerate a mass of one kilogram one meter per second per second, equal to 100,000 dynes.
Pascal	Pa	A unit of pressure equal to one Newton per square meter.
Planck's constant	h	The constant of proportionality relating the energy of a photon to the frequency of that photon. It value is approximately 6.626×10^{-34} joule-second
Speed of light	c	In vacuum is equal to 2.998×10^{10} cm s^{-1} or 2.998×10^{5} Km s^{-1} or $1.863 \ 10^{5}$ miles per second.
Torr	$torr$	A unit of pressure that is equal to approximately 1.316×10^{-3} atmosphere or 1,333 pascals.

GLOSSARY OF COMMON SYMBOLS AND ABBREVIATIONS

ADP/O ratio: Number of molecules of ADP phosphorylated to ATP per atom of O_2 reduced to water.

ATP/O ratio: Number of molecules of ATP formed per atom of O_2 reduced to water.

Mass: A unified body of matter with no specific shape. A physical substance; the universe as a whole.

E: energy: Force, strength or active power. The capacity of a physical system to do work. The units of work are identical to those of energy.

The principle that a measured quantity of energy is equivalent to a measure quantity of mass is expressed by the following Einstein's equations: $E = mc^2$, where m = mass and c = velocity of light.

Kinetic energy: The energy possessed by a body because of its motion, equal to one half the mass of the body times the square of its speed.

$E = \frac{1}{2} mv^2$, where m is the mass of the object and v^2 is the speed multiplied by itself. The value of E can also be derived from the abbreviation *(ma)d*, where a is the acceleration applied to the mass, m, and d the distance through which a acts.

119

Potential energy:	The energy of a particle or system of particles derived from position or condition, rather than motion. Work is needed to give a system potential energy, and a system's potential energy is equal to the work done on the system.
Internal energy (U):	The total kinetic and potential energy associated with the motions and relative positions of the molecules of an object, excluding the kinetic or potential energy of the object as a whole. Change in internal energy ΔU, approximately equal to ΔE E_h: Standard redox potential. The numerical values of the *reduction potential* relative to the $2H^+ + 2e^- = H_2$ half-reaction which is taken as -0.414 volt at pH 7. The value for the hydrogen half-reaction at pH 7 was calculated from the arbitrarily assigned value of $E^o = 0.0$ volts under true standard-state conditions of 1 M H^+ and 1 atmosphere H_2.
ΔE_h:	Difference in redox potential in mV between two carriers of reducing Equivalents
$\Delta E^{o'}$:	The change in standard redox potential for the half reaction is + 0.82V for water formation ($\frac{1}{2} O_2 + 2H^+ + 2e^- = H_2O$) and -0.320 V for NADH formation ($NAD^+ + 2H^+ + 2e^- + NADH$)
	$\Delta E^{o'} = [\Delta E^{o'}$ **of the half-reaction containing the oxidizing agent]**
	- [$\Delta E^{o'}$ of the half-reaction containing the reducing agent]
	$\Delta E^{o'}$ values may be thought of as electron pressures and, as such, they are independent of the number of electrons in the half-reaction reaction.
E_m:	Membrane potential. Energy made available by a concentration gradient of ions or electrons across a membrane (with the inside negative relative to the outside). At a pH gradient of 1.4 units the membrane potential is of 0.14 volts positive outside. By convention the resting membrane potential is written with a minus sign.

$\Delta\psi = \Delta E_m$:	Difference in electrical potential across the mitochondrial inner-membrane in volts.
G:	Gibbs free energy. Energy released or utilized in a chemical reaction
ΔG:	Difference in free energy. A thermodynamic quantity, equal to the difference between energy contents of products and reactants.

$$\Delta G = 2.303RT \log C_2 / C_1 + ZF\Delta\Psi$$

ΔG^o:	The free energy change under standard-state conditions in which all reactants and products are considered to be maintained at *steady- state concentrations* of 1 M and the standard-state for gases is considered to be 1 atmosphere in partial pressure.
$\Delta G^{o'}$:	Standard free-energy change under conditions in which the pH is 7.0.
Gp:	Phosphorylation potential. A measure of the energy status of the cell that is defined by the following molar ratio: [ATP] / [ADP] [P_i]
ΔGp:	Difference in phosphorylation potential defined as the free energy required for ATP synthesis: $\Delta Gp = \Delta G^o + RT \ln ([ATP] / [ADP] [Pi])$.
H: Enthalpy:	A thermodynamic function of a system, equivalent to the sum of the internal energy of the system plus the product of its volume multiplied by the pressure exerted on it by the surroundings.

$$H = E + PV$$

ΔH:	Change in enthalpy or heat content of the system. Represents the quantity of heat released (or absorbed) at constant temperature, pressure and volume. Since in all biochemical reactions the volume change, ΔV, is very small, the change in enthalpy is practical equal to the change in internal energy: $\Delta H = \Delta E$:

Δp:	Proton motive force across the mitochondrial membrane
S:	Entropy. A quantitative measure of the amount of thermal energy not available to do work in a closed thermodynamic system
ΔS:	Entropy change. Change in disorder or randomness in a closed system. he product of temperature and ΔS is equal to the product of the change in enthalpy and proton-motive force: $T\Delta S = \Delta H \, x \, \Delta p$.
ΔpH:	Change in chemical potential of protons. The change in the chemical component of Δp is equal to 0.084 V (1.4 units lower outside than inside).

SUBJECT INDEX